Anorexics on Anorexia

of related interest

Arts Therapies and Clients with Eating Disorders
Fragile Board
Edited by Ditty Dokter
ISBN 1 85302 256 X

Figures of Lightness
Anorexia, Bulimia and Psychoanalysis
Gabriella Ripa di Meana
ISBN 1 85302 617 4

Anorexics on Anorexia

Edited by Rosemary Shelley

Jessica Kingsley Publishers
London and Bristol, Pennsylvania

The right of the contributors to be identified as authors of this work has been asserted by them in accordance with the Copyright, Designs and Patents Act 1988.

This edition first published in the United Kingdom in 1997 by
Jessica Kingsley Publishers Ltd,
116 Pentonville Road,
London N1 9JB,
England
and
325 Chestnut Street,
Philadelphia, PA 19106, USA.

www.jkp.com

Second impression 1999

Copyright © 1997 Jessica Kingsley Publishers

Library of Congress Cataloging in Publication Data
A CIP catalogue record for this book is available from the Library of Congress

British Library Cataloguing in Publication Data
A CIP catalogue record for this book is available from the British Library

ISBN 1-85302-471-6

Printed and Bound in Great Britain by
Athenaeum Press, Gateshead, Tyne and Wear

In Memory of Catherine

Acknowledgements

All credit for the publication of this book must go to its contributors. Mine was the idea; they were the ones who put in the hard work. I thank them most sincerely for having the courage to write about their experiences. I hope they gained something from it. I also thank Jessica Kingsley Publishers for giving me the opportunity to produce a book so desperately needed in the field of eating disorders. I thank my lovely family – Mum, Dad, Peter, Andrew and Suzanne for putting up with years of hell and never giving up on me. I hope the publication of this book makes some of our struggle worthwhile. Thanks to Peter for proofreading the manuscript. Last, but certainly not least, my sincere thanks must go to Bonnie, my psychotherapist, without whom I would not be alive today. Thank you, Bonnie, for your exceptional patience, kindness and perseverance.

Contents

The contributors to this volume include:

Rachel Ashton
Simon Brooks
Callum Cochrane
Fiona M. Cowan
Claire Empson
Sue Evan-Jones
Sheila E. Fraser
Sandra Jackson
June Johnson
Yvonne Johnston
Bernadette Keane
Jean Menzies-Welham
Valerie Sims
Delphine Elizabeth Williams
Catherine

Introduction

There is no easy way to introduce a book that tells of so much suffering yet offers so much hope. *Anorexics on Anorexia* gives the stories of 19 sufferers, all at different stages in their recovery. Although their experiences are, in parts, harrowing and moving, these people have all made progress. This book is about survival, often against the odds. It shows that recovery from Anorexia Nervosa, though not easy, is possible. That is an important message for sufferers, their families and carers to hear.

The main reason I put this book together was that when I was ill myself it was the type of book I looked for. I wanted to know what Anorexia was really like, not through the eyes of the medical professionals, but in the words of those people who had experienced the illness themselves. I wanted to know that I was not alone, and that I was not odd or unusual. I wanted to find reasons behind my behaviour, but more importantly I wanted to know that Anorexia could be survived. I never found that book, so I decided to put one together myself. *Anorexics on Anorexia* is the result.

I have not, of course, put this book together alone. All credit has to go to the sufferers who have provided me with their accounts. Although they all have an anorexic history in common their similarities end there. Their individual experiences of the illness are all unique. Each chapter provides the reader with a different message and offers a different angle on anorexic suffering.

Anorexia is not an illness experienced just by teenage girls and the contributors to this book reflect that. They represent a cross-section of sufferers from pre-adolescence to middle age and beyond. There are accounts from both males and females. They speak of different treatment methods, some effective, others highly ineffective and even damaging. The different issues, problems, worries and traumas that triggered the onset of their eating problems are also analysed in detail.

These include bullying, divorce within the family, rape and sexual abuse, the death of a close friend or relative, media pressure, alcoholism and emotional neglect.

Each contributor has relived their suffering in order to share their experiences with others and prove that there can be life after Anorexia. The aim of this book is to increase knowledge, understanding and awareness of Anorexia Nervosa in the minds of those people with an interest in this field of mental health in a professional capacity or as a family member or close friend of a sufferer. More importantly, however, this book has been written for those suffering from the illness. Anorexia is a highly complex problem that is often difficult to understand especially for those going through it. This book aims to unravel some of that confusion and help sufferers to understand themselves and their behaviour more fully. My hope is that this will bring about changes in behaviour that point them in the direction of recovery.

This book is dedicated to Catherine Dunbar. I read Catherine's story in a book written by her mother Maureen (Dunbar 1987). That book gave me so much insight and a greater level of understanding of Anorexia. It made me realise just how dangerous the illness can be. Catherine, sadly, died at the age of twenty-two. Her story gave me the determination and courage to fight Anorexia, to fight the voice in my head that told me I was fat and did not deserve to eat. It shocked me into realising that Anorexia was not a game, it was a serious life-threatening illness that had a devastating effect on sufferers, all those that know them, and all those that read about them. I knew that Catherine would have wanted me to fight, and so with that thought in mind, I did. I wish I could thank Catherine for the strength she gave me.

No one can speak more effectively about the illness than those people that have been through it; they are the 'experts' so I leave them to tell their own stories in their own words. It would be impossible to summarise their experiences, however there are several issues and themes that seem fairly constant throughout.

Comparing the accounts of anorexics who first fell ill in the 1950s and 1960s with those of today it is clear that medical knowledge in the field of eating disorders has greatly improved. However, advancements still need to be made. Too many hospitalised sufferers are being treated in ways that have proved to be detrimental to their long-term

physical and mental health. This is particularly the case when anorexics
are fed vast amounts of food to produce rapid weight gain that they are
unable to cope with mentally and subsequently lose on discharge from
hospital. In the words of one sufferer:

> What really surprised and shocked me was the fact that the focus
> was on feeding me up to produce a change in my body, but never
> once did they take my mind into consideration. The way I was
> feeling did not seem important to them. I received very little in
> the way of counselling. (Fiona)

The emphasis in this method of treatment, and one commonly used, it
seems, is clearly on the patient's physical condition and the urgent need
for weight to be increased. However the patient's mental condition is
often overlooked. This should not be the case. Anorexia Nervosa is,
after all, a mental illness.

A period of hospitalisation, if not effectively handled by the medical
care team, can be detrimental to the patient's health in other ways too.
If the sufferer is placed on a ward with other anorexics, which is often
unavoidable, then a high level of competitiveness can develop between
the patients. They can battle with each other to be the one that eats the
least and loses the most weight. The competition can be positive at
times but supportive staff need to be aware of its negative effects also.

One contributor speaks of being admitted to hospital with Anorexia
and being very naive about the illness. However by the time she left
she termed herself an 'expert.' During her admission period she had
learnt how to hide food, to artificially increase her weight on weigh
days, and even how to vomit after meals. All this she learnt from the
other anorexics she was in hospital with. This level of 'collusion'
between sufferers must therefore be avoided as much as possible.

Speaking of her first experience of hospitalisation, and her relationship with other anorexics, Kate says:

> We would compete with each other at the dining table but the
> rest of the time we were the best of friends and would collude
> with each other's behaviour. One would often keep guard while
> the others went out jogging. We would hide each other's food
> and back each other up if someone was lying to the staff. (Kate)

It is also evident that the earlier a person's Anorexia is noticed, diagnosed and effectively treated, the shorter the period of recovery and the better the long-term prognosis. However, it is a sad fact that anorexics, in many cases, are still not receiving the treatment they need at the time they need it. Treating anorexics whose weight has reached a dangerous level is all very well but for many sufferers that level of descent into the illness could have been avoided with effective treatment in the initial stages.

Contributors speak of being sent away by their GPs, after initially presenting them with their food problems, and being told to 'Go home and eat' or 'Go for a walk around the garden'. If only it were that simple. To admit to having an eating problem, having the courage to seek medical help, but then being sent away with nothing is humiliating and even fatal.

Joanne has been ill for 30 years. She is 40 years old, currently in hospital being tube-fed and weighing less than four stone. She writes:

> I feel the underlying reason for why I am as I am today is that I was left to fester too long. I believe that if I had received treatment years ago I would have conquered Anorexia by now. (Joanne)

The sufferers identify several different factors that have contributed to their Anorexia. There is no single cause. For many it was the result of a number of different factors that had built up over time. For the sufferer with constant worries and concerns Anorexia can focus their thoughts elsewhere, thus serving to reduce the significance of these underlying issues. A starving body becomes preoccupied with food, eventually to the extent that little else enters the mind. Life eventually revolves around food and weight and nothing else matters.

> Anorexia crept up on me slowly and relentlessly – eventually becoming the driving force behind my whole existence. (Victoria)

> I counted every single calorie I consumed. I was totally and utterly wrapped up in my dieting, my weight and image. Nothing else mattered. (Fiona)

Anorexia can persist when the anorexic gains something from being ill. Not only can a preoccupation with food block out problems, worries and concerns, but it can also gain the sufferer attention they felt previously deprived of and desperately needed. It is hard to ignore a person who refuses to eat and who is rapidly losing weight. Although the attention is negative attention, for many it is seen as preferable to no attention at all.

A starving adult or child can also shift the focus of a family away from one particular member, such as an alcoholic mother or an abusive father, and onto the anorexic instead. The anorexic becomes 'the problem'. In Carla's story her parents were persistently arguing. Carla stopped eating and their attention shifted to her situation instead. This served to reduce their arguing and focus their attentions on her instead.

> The longer I did not eat the more attention my parents gave me and the less time they spent arguing. I felt happier because they were not so angry with each other all the time but I was worried that if I ate they would stop looking after me and would start arguing again. Since they had become concerned about me they had stopped fighting. It therefore seemed like my job to keep them together. (Carla)

The anorexic has the power to disrupt family life completely and considerably alter its functioning.

> The family plays a part in Anorexia, they are not necessarily the cause, but just as you suffer with it, they suffer too. Their frustration is that there is little they can do in altering the course of the illness. Families are like spectators in the front row, too close for comfort, encouraging and applauding when they do not understand the underlying plot. (Jean)

> My family had practically been torn apart by the illness. For my baby sister, growing up in such a sick environment, ill health, arguments and extreme tension were all she knew. She developed a stammer at the age of four because she was so permanently anxious. (Kate)

Anorexia can also provide the sufferers with a high level of control over their lives – control they may never have experienced before. For the first time they may also gain control over their friends or family and gain the power to change the course of situations where previously they felt powerless to do so. Anorexics may find that their problems are out of their control, but by controlling their food intake they at least have control over something. Anorexia can also provide a focus in life. Weight loss can be viewed as an achievement producing a sense of pride and self-esteem previously lacked.

> My problems seemed out of my control but what I ate and what I weighed was within my control. It also gave me a sense of achievement and enjoyment. I hated life at school and I hated life at home. But what I did enjoy was losing weight. (Helen)

> I found a great sense of achievement in being able to refuse all the 'fattening' foods I was offered. It put me on a tremendous high. This elation made all the periods of intense starvation worthwhile. (Simon)

Anorexia can be so difficult to give up because of these benefits to the sufferers. Also, weight loss and the fasting high that starvation produces can be addictive. Giving up Anorexia has been compared with giving up heroin and coming off alcohol.

> There was no real reason why I wanted to lose weight. I think I had become addicted to it – addicted to the high I got from starvation and from seeing the scales go down and down. (Elaine)

The illness also traps the sufferer in a vicious circle of starvation and weight loss. Starving the body inevitably starves the mind. This can result in a lack of reasoning and common sense.

> ...my body was so severely undernourished it was obvious that there was no possible way my mind could think straight. (Fiona)

> I fully understand how illogical it must seem to starve yourself to near death. But Anorexia is not a concern of logic. (Jean)

> Your mind has complete control over your whole body; your powers of reasoning are gone; logic and common sense are non-existent. (Callum)

Anorexia greatly alters the personality of the sufferer. The anorexic becomes egotistical, aggressive, deceitful, dishonest, secretive and even violent. This can considerably distress close friends and family members. Some relationships can be destroyed and significant people lost. This, as well as the anorexic's avoidance of social situations for fear of having to eat or drink, further isolates the sufferer.

> ...my social life had collapsed. I religiously avoided all social events. Spending time with other people invariably meant eating and drinking with them, and besides, seeing people eat disgusted me. (Victoria)

The anorexic can quickly reach the stage when all they have left in their lives is their Anorexia. It then becomes even more difficult to give it up as the sufferer's perception is that they will be left with nothing.

Anorexics are highly sensitive people although at times they will appear far from sensitive in their treatment of other people. Sufferers will become aware, at some stage, of the extent to which their illness has affected others. This knowledge will further add to their self-hate and feelings of worthlessness. This can serve to reinforce the starvation and hence the Anorexia. The result: yet another vicious circle.

An important point that I hope readers pick up from this book is that although Anorexia can benefit the sufferer in certain ways these benefits are short-lived. It is not long before the depression sets in and physical complications add to the level of distress. The contributors identify a number of physical ailments suffered as a direct result of starvation. I list them here in the hope that it will deter others from travelling down the path of Anorexia. For those already ill I hope it will shock them into finding the determination to fight their illness and find within themselves the will to live. Just some of those physical complications are osteoporosis, infertility, feelings of extreme cold and weakness, severe sleep disturbances, cramp, and major organ failure.

> As I hovered towards the five stone marker my front teeth started to feel loose. That was it – I realised I was in trouble and suddenly became aware of the fact that unless I got help I would die. (Victoria)

The prospect of weight gain is made increasingly traumatic for anorexics by the fact that many cannot visibly see the extent of their emaciation. No matter what weight the sufferer is, the feelings of being fat still remain. So as anorexics never feel thin they will always strive to be thinner to such an extent that people have died still believing they were fat.

> It is like looking in one of those funny mirrors at a funfair that totally distorts your reflection. Except with Anorexia you can't just walk away from it (Callum)

If the picture I have painted here of Anorexia is distressing and bleak then I make no apologies. To suffer with Anorexia Nervosa *is* distressing and bleak. The horror of the illness and the level of suffering should never be underestimated. It is a highly dangerous illness and so much more careful attention needs to be paid to it and more help offered. The more positive news is that people do recover. Some recover completely; others only partially recover but are still able to lead fulfilling lives.

The method of recovery is as unique as the individual sufferer and the set of problems that contributed to the onset of the illness in the first place. Some sufferers need a hospital admission but the majority of sufferers are able to recover without inpatient treatment through the use of various other facilities available including day patient or outpatient hospital treatment, self-help, local support groups, individual and group psychotherapy and family therapy. A wide range of therapeutic approaches have proved beneficial for eating disorder sufferers. These include self-awareness groups, body image groups, transactional analysis and assertiveness training. Support services available through GPs can include dietitians, counsellors and community mental health teams.

The Eating Disorder Association provides members with details of local support groups as well as counsellors and postal contacts. They also offer information and understanding through telephone helplines and newsletters. A highly recommended book is *Anorexia Nervosa – The Wish to Change* (1996) by Crisp, Joughin, Halek and Bowyer which details their thirty-step self-help programme. In her book *Arts Therapies and Clients with Eating Disorders* (1994), Ditty Dokter highlights the benefits of the arts therapies as part of a multi-diciplinary approach. The arts therapies have played an increasingly important role in the treatment of eating disorders in recent years. They include art therapy, music therapy, drama therapy and dance movement therapy and are particularly useful for sufferers who have difficulty expressing themselves verbally. They enable sufferers to explore feelings and emotions in a safe environment using creativity and musical improvisation. Arts therapies can replace food as a transactional object and form of self-expression. They can also communicate a large amount of subconscious information through the sufferer's use of colour, space, sound and movement which the therapist can interpret and then discuss with the individual.

Anorexics are extremely focused, determined and strong-willed individuals. With help, support and use of their own resources, most sufferers can reverse the downward spiral of weight loss and break out of the interlocking vicious circles that trap them. It is, however, crucial that sufferers attempt to build up a reliable support network of family, friends and professionals offering support and encouragement. Recovery from Anorexia Nervosa isn't easy but it *is* possible. *Anorexics on Anorexia* is evidence of that.

I hope this book will increase the knowledge and understanding in society of eating disorders in general and Anorexia Nervosa in particular, of its complexity and severity. I hope for improvements in treatment methods where treatment is needed. I also hope that sufferers are able to appreciate that Anorexia results in their losing more than just weight, and that no one deserves to endure the torture of starvation, no matter how they feel about themselves. I hope it can save people from experiencing the horror that is Anorexia Nervosa.

References

Dokter, D. (1994) *Arts Therapies and Clients with Eating Disorders: Fragile Board.* London: Jessica Kingsley Publishers.

Crisp, A.H., Joughin, N., Halek, C. And Bowyer, C. (1996) *Anorexia Nervosa – The Wish to Change.* London: Psychology Press.

Dunbar, M. (1987) *Catherine, A Tragic Life.* London: Penguin Books.

CHAPTER 1

Anorexic Anger

'Why feed a body that doesn't want to live?'

Kate, now 23, is able to look back on her experience of Anorexia with fresh insight and intellectualise all that happened to her during the seven painful years she suffered with the illness. This has helped her greatly because Anorexia can seem a confusing illness, especially to those coming through it. Through counselling and her own self-reflection Kate has been able to piece together exactly what was going on for her at the time of her illness. She speaks very much of Anorexia being her coping mechanism, something she needed in order to live, but with it she nearly died. At the time she was unable to see the irony of it all. Now, however, the situation is different. Here Kate tells her story…

Anorexia nearly killed me; it also saved my life. To most people that statement would not make sense but in fact it is not as contradictory as it might at first sound. Although the illness made me extremely ill, I could not have coped with life without it. Anorexia was my coping mechanism. Without it I would have given up many years ago. I certainly would not be here today. Thank goodness I am; I have so much to live for now. But back then life seemed very different.

I developed Anorexia at the age of 15. In the year before I became ill my life was one of complete misery and severe depression. I hated school and the pressure of forthcoming exams and I was arguing with my parents a lot. But more than anything I hated myself. I was also convinced that everybody hated me. I realise now that with my low mood had come a touch of paranoia. Because I disliked myself so much it seemed absolutely impossible that anyone else would like me. I managed to convince myself that the world was against me, that they talked about me behind my back and that no one wanted to be my friend. I was also a perfectionist. I wanted to be the best, at everything and immediately. It bothered me greatly that it took time to learn things so at school I became increasingly frustrated. I wanted to know everything and I wanted to know it *now*. I felt that there was pressure from home too. My parents, naturally, wanted me to do well. Every time my grades slipped just a little I felt extremely guilty and felt that I had let them down terribly. I hated myself for that.

I danced a lot too and for years I enjoyed it. But I was not the best at everything so I decided that I was not good enough, I had failed again, I was worthless and pathetic, and I was ugly. As I became more depressed I started scrutinising my body in the mirror more. I did not like what I saw. I became convinced that I was fatter than every one else and began to reduce my food intake.

I reached the point where I really did not care about anything anymore and so I stopped eating completely. Why feed a body that doesn't want to live? To me food was life and I simply did not want to be alive. My intention from the very beginning was to starve to death and I was absolutely determined that that was exactly what I would do. It was not a case of 'if' I died but rather 'when'. I calmed down a little then, once I had made the decision to die; I knew it would take time and I knew I had to be patient. I knew the suffering would end one day and I was prepared to wait. I gave up the dancing. Not surprisingly I had become too weak to take part in one class a week let alone twenty. I also dropped out of my 'A' level classes and left school. It was obvious to everyone that something was very wrong with me but no one knew exactly what it was. It was clear that I was stressed and that my personality had changed, that I had become more introverted and withdrawn, but no one knew why. I don't think I was even sure myself. All that I knew was that the world had suddenly become a horrible place to live in.

However I suddenly noticed one day that my mood had lifted considerably. I no longer felt as depressed as usual and in fact life didn't seem so bad after all. Starvation seemed the answer to everything – life had become so much easier since I had stopped eating. I wished I had thought of it sooner. I honestly feel, looking back, that this uplift in mood was partly to do with the fact that I thought I was going to die and that my life on this earth would soon be over. I also suspect, however, due to the knowledge I now have, that I was on a 'fasting high'. Life was great; I was floating on air without a care in the world.

Previously so much had worried me: poverty, famine, cancer, death, war, disease. The list was endless, as was the anxiety, but miraculously it had all vanished and all that occupied my thoughts was food. Food quickly became the main focus of my life. It was as if nothing else mattered.

Many people asked me how starving could be the answer to my problems and, somewhat naively at the time, I would give the following example. If we imagine, hypothetically speaking, that the average person is preoccupied with food 20 per cent of their day then they spend the remaining 80 per cent thinking and worrying about other things. A starving person will think about the one thing their body desperately needs and that is food. So their preoccupation increases to say, 30 per cent. The lower the weight and the more severe the state of starvation the higher the level of preoccupation with food until eventually, at a state of extreme emaciation, the level is nearer 90–100 per cent. This leaves no time, energy or space in the mind to think about anything else and so the problems of the world disappear. They have been pushed out by food. Simple. Straightforward. Easy.

After a while my mother insisted I went to the doctor and I agreed to go. I know that even then there was a part of me that wanted help and wanted to sort out my life. I could have flatly refused to attend the appointment but I didn't. My mother came in to see the doctor with me knowing that I was not likely to tell him anything if I was on my own. She explained that she had noticed that I had not been eating properly. A brief chat followed and his words of advice were to 'Go for a walk around the garden'. I couldn't believe it. I was absolutely furious and I felt highly insulted. I felt like a complete fake and that there was nothing wrong with me after all. I knew that there was, but how could I get other people to believe me if a doctor had given me the all clear? I was outraged and more determined than ever to starve myself to death. I was determined that it would be the last time I tried to seek help. It still angers me now to think of that appointment. I am aware that at that stage I was not so far into the Anorexia that I could not be helped. In fact I strongly believe that it is at the early stages of the illness that the sufferer can best be helped. When behaviour patterns become more ingrained they become more difficult to change, especially as weight loss distorts the thinking process and it is even more difficult to rationalise in your own mind why you should bother at all.

By the time my condition was taken seriously, and I eventually did get an appointment with a psychiatrist, it was too late. I was just too ill mentally and I no longer wanted help. I was too deep into my Anorexia and the illness had completely taken me over. I felt in complete control and I did not want that taken away from me. My personality had also changed. Looking back it is clear that the kind, polite, friendly Kate had gone. A deceitful, dishonest, manipulative anorexic had taken her place.

I continued starving and the weight rapidly fell off. At that point things began to look brighter; I chose a new school to go to and different 'A' level subjects. After a year away I was starting to feel bored and in need of some academic stimulation. I was six and a half stone when I joined the new school. At the time I thought that no one knew about my illness. I found out years later that everyone had known. Many had heard that an 'anorexic girl' would be joining the school, and others had known I had a problem the moment they saw me. Apparently it was obvious, but not to me.

Life continued smoothly I felt, though my family and immediate friends might have thought otherwise. I was locked in my own world and as long as I was not eating and as long as I was constantly losing weight then I was happy. I was not really in touch with the outside world to any great degree. Looking back now I am aware that I became very egotistical. I thought I existed in isolation. I gave very little thought to the people around me that I was affecting, my friends and my family, the people I loved so much. The day those people threatened the safety of my Anorexia world, with my anorexic thoughts and my anorexic friends, was the day they became the enemy. To me they did not understand. This was my world, my life, my illness. Couldn't they see that I needed it? Why were they trying to take it away from me? By trying to encourage me to eat they were threatening my very existence and putting my life in danger. I needed Anorexia to live. They thought that if I had it I would die. I was convinced that my ideas were right and that everyone else was wrong. I am certain my thought processes must have become very distorted. I was six stone at a height of five foot five inches and I was convinced that I was fat; no one could have convinced me otherwise. Now I see how distorted my thinking was but there was no way that I could have seen that at the time – I was too ill, and too wrapped up in the illness. As far as I was concerned I had too much to gain from it even to think of listening to what other people were saying to me – never mind thinking of giving it up.

My friends and family were the enemy but it was the professionals that had the weapons. They had the power to put me in hospital but I was determined not to let that happen. I was dragged off to see counsellors, psychologists and more psychiatrists. It all became a game to me although I was not having fun at all; it was all starting to become one long nightmare. The depression had returned with a vengeance. It was so much worse than before. I was very cold and permanently tired which made matters worse. I would wear layers and layers of clothes even in the heat of summer. To me it felt like one long permanent winter, not just cold but bleak and miserable too. I couldn't sleep at night either and that left me grumpy and irritable. I was constantly rude to people and very aggressive. I was angry, with life, with everything.

The doctors were making matters worse. Their constant threat of hospitalisation made me highly deceitful as I had to pretend my weight was higher than it actually was. I would drink bottles of water before I was weighed and hide weights in my pockets. It worked for a while until the morning I was caught out. I overslept and so when my mother weighed me I was five and a half stone. By that afternoon I was in an Adolescent Unit. I hated it at first, people trying to make me eat all the time, but then I settled in and made friends. There were lots of other anorexics there to join my world, and they did. We would compete with each other at the dining table but the rest of the time we were the best of friends and would collude with each others behaviour. One would often keep guard while the others went out jogging. We would hide each other's food and back each other up if someone was lying to the staff. It was really pathetic behaviour for someone who by the time they were discharged was 19 years old and only ten pounds heavier.

Many more hospital admissions followed which was hardly surprising since I had no intention of ever getting better and so it was inevitable that while living in the outside world I would not eat and so would lose weight. Being in hospital became like Anorexia – a very safe, sheltered existence – and apart from the meals and the resulting weight gain I enjoyed it. I don't think I was so desperate to die anymore, I just wanted to remain living in that world.

It wasn't until years later that things began to change. I found a counsellor that I grew really to like and respect. She was living in the 'outside world' and I connected with her on an emotional level. That meant I was becoming in touch with reality. My counsellor genuinely wanted me to get better and I could see that. At first I wanted to get better for her, then I realised I had to do it for myself as well. I would often test how much my counsellor cared by losing lots of weight to see what her reaction was. It was always one of concern to begin with and later annoyance and desperation. She stuck with me during the hospital admissions that followed. As a result of that she passed the test and I made the very conscious decision to get better.

It was not as easy as I thought. I had to learn a whole new way of living. Life as a normal-weight, healthy adult was something I had never experienced before and I was not sure I wanted to. Gaining weight was hell and I often felt extremely desperate at times to the point of giving up, but something kept me going, some sort of 'life-force' as my counsellor called it. The opposing death-force was still there but it was fighting a losing battle. I soon reached the stage where I was 'sitting on the fence' – I was not seriously ill with Anorexia but then I was not completely well either. I was nowhere really and so not surprisingly I felt as if I could not relate to anyone and I just did not fit in anywhere. That was the point when I had to decide which way to go – back into the safety of Anorexia or further along the path of recovery and into the unknown where all that was certain was that I did not have the illness to help me cope, that I was on my own. But that was it, I wasn't on my own, I had come to realise that there were people there for me, my family and my counsellor. I had lost a lot of my friends as I had neglected them during the course of my illness but as my condition improved some of them came back.

It was only when I had gained nearly two stone in weight that I started to realise what Anorexia had cost me, my friends for one thing. I was lucky to get them back. I also realised at that stage how my illness had affected the people around me, in particular the people that had to live with my agony day in day out. My family had practically been torn apart by the illness. For my baby sister, growing up in such a sick environment, ill health, arguments and extreme tension were all she knew. She developed a stammer at the age of four because she was so permanently anxious.

She is much happier now but I will always be angry with myself for neglecting the responsibility I had as a sister and family member. I treated everyone so badly but if I dwell on that too much I'll get ill again. I'll start punishing myself by starving. It did not hurt physically in the initial stages of the illness but now it does. I do not think I could starve again, not to that extent, even if I wanted to. At one time that thought would have been unbearable; now I think it's a good thing.

I have left Anorexia behind now and I never want to go back to it again but I do miss it at times. I miss the security it gave me, the security of knowing what every day would be like. It would be miserable and painful but at least it would be predictable. There seemed so much less to worry about then, just food and weight, nothing else. Now I have feelings again and the world is a much more real place. That isn't always easy to deal with. I'm 23 now but I feel as if I am still 15 emotionally, the age I was when I developed Anorexia. I seemed to have become stuck at that age but I am aware that I am very slowly growing up. I have picked up where I left off but that isn't easy when people expect me to be so much older than I feel I really am. I can put on the professional front and I do it well, but that's not the real me, the real me is still developing. I still suffer the physical side effects – sore knee joints, extreme exhaustion, irregular heartbeat at times – but that is just something I have to live with; at least I am alive. My views on the illness have changed considerably. At one time I thought that I had made a conscious decision one day to stop eating. Now I realise that that was not the case at all. For me the illness developed very gradually over a long period of time. Giving up food was not something that happened overnight; it wasn't something I even decided to do. It just happened.

The illness progressed because I felt I gained something from it; now I realise that I lost so much. I lost seven years of my life that I will never regain and that is sad. I was also extremely selfish. I can now appreciate all the pain and anguish I caused other people. My memories of the illness are horrific and are likely never to go away but what they will do is remind me why I should never relapse.

I had an illness; I wasn't 'misbehaving' or 'acting out' as some people might say. That thought reduces the self-hate to an extent. It may be wrong to blame my behaviour on the fact that I was ill but it does help to explain it to an extent. Anorexia turned me into a very nasty, dishonest, deceitful person. That was not the real me. I thought I was in control of my life when I was anorexic but in fact I was not in control at all. The illness was in control of me. It was gradually destroying me and I didn't even realise it. It was still a very effective coping mechanism and I will still say that it saved my life but it nearly killed me too. I hope that statement makes more sense now.

CHAPTER 2

The Safety and Secrecy of the Anorexic World

'The aim of the treatment seemed to be a case
of fattening me up and sending me home.'

*Fiona's story raises many points, one of which refers to the inpatient treatment
of anorexics. Fiona uses the expression 'eating myself out of hospital' and this
is something that many anorexics do. This, in the long run, is extremely
unhelpful and any anorexic who gains weight just to be discharged from
hospital is very likely to relapse very quickly. As Fiona's story shows, when
treating Anorexia it is not just the sufferer's physical condition that needs to
be considered but their mental state too. This, after all, is a mental illness.
However even with today's level of medical knowledge this single point, a
point crucial to the successful treatment of eating disorders, is being
overlooked.*

Let me begin by taking you back almost 16 years to the beginning of
my illness. Looking back on my life many would say I had the perfect
childhood. I had a mother, father, older brother and a very comfortable
lifestyle. My father was my headmaster at secondary school and my
mother had a part-time job although she didn't really need to work. I
was such a happy child – perfect to bring up, my mother said.

At the age of 17 all that changed. I had always been a plump child
– 'puppy fat' I was told. At the beginning of secondary school I wore
a size 16 school skirt, weighed over nine and a half stone and could
eat, in any day, the equivalent of my overweight father. By the sixth

year I'd decided that I had had enough – the torment I had endured for years from the other pupils was taking its toll. I decided to diet and step up the will-power. It was not too long and was quite encouraging when I soon dropped to a size eight and was receiving more positive comments about my shape.

At this point in time I'd never thought that there was anything wrong about what was happening to me. As far as I was concerned I was simply on a diet and nothing more. I was also pleased that for the first time in my life I could sustain this will-power. However it was not too long before my parents started noticing my avoidance of food. Mealtimes were becoming increasingly difficult and any opportunity to miss a meal was a temptation. I'd continually say I was full or that I had eaten earlier. I'd try any excuse not to eat.

I was eventually taken to the family doctor and that was when the trouble began. He asked my father if I was in fact capable of eating a proper meal. He was clearly concerned about my condition and as he examined me he commented that my ribs were sticking out. That resulted, on returning home, in an angry lecture from my father. I felt bad for upsetting him and felt forced to ease off the will-power a little. I was too frightened to anger him. Although I was the 'apple of his eye' and loved him dearly, I would never argue with him.

Tragedy struck my family in May 1981 when my father suffered a massive heart attack and died suddenly. Naturally we were all devastated. We wondered how such a thing could have happened to us. I was only 17 and my father was 47. It seemed such a waste of a life. He was such a popular, well-known and recognised figure in our neighbourhood. We just could not believe or take in that he had passed away so unexpectedly. Being the family we are we all tended to hide our feelings and emotions and were 'brave' for each other. To this day I have never really spoken to my brother about what it was like to find my dead father lying in the chair. As the weeks went by I seemed to take charge of the family; I felt I adopted my father's role in a way. As long as my mother and brother were coping it did not matter about me. I told myself that I was strong, that I could cope. That's what I thought. Everything seemed like one long nightmare. I kept convincing myself that one day I would wake up from it.

I had applied to a Physical Education College. My application had been accepted but then I failed the only exam I needed to pass in order to gain a place. I remember feeling such a failure – I kept asking myself what my father would have thought if he had been alive. He too had been a teacher and I desperately wanted to follow in his footsteps. I had set my heart on this course. I remember fasting for weeks after that – possibly as a punishment. Eventually I did pass the exam and at last I could set off for my four-year course in Edinburgh. That is when I feel the real problems began.

I weighed around eight and a half stone, and at five foot six inches was reasonably healthy. I remember the first lecture we were given by the college doctor. She claimed that all students usually put on between one and two stones in their first year. She also spoke about Anorexia and said that there seemed to be 'one' in each year. Little did I know at the time what lay ahead!

I was incredibly homesick to begin with and thought a lot about my mother. I developed numerous injuries as a result of all the sport I did. One injury resulted in plaster – a fractured leg and a badly torn ligament. I was so depressed and concerned that my studies would be affected that once again I started cutting down on my food intake. My weight was seven stone nine pounds but was rapidly dropping. It was not too long before the college doctor summoned me to her surgery. She said that she was planning to refer me to a hospital psychiatrist as an outpatient although she was in fact determined to do all in her power to get me admitted. She feared that things had already got out of hand and because of the demands of my course was concerned about my physical health which had deteriorated significantly. I agreed to see someone on a weekly basis and that for a while stabilised things. I continued from there to seek further help.

The remaining three years at college were up and down, some better than others, although every day was a constant struggle with food. I had such will-power that I knew I would make the end of my course and manage to survive in the safety and secrecy of my anorexic world. In the final year my weight was around seven stone two pounds and for a year I ate in the seclusion of my college bedroom. Eating with people had become a problem and too much of an ordeal – it seemed so much easier to eat by myself.

Eventually I graduated and in 1987 I got my first job. Being the typical perfectionist I am I worked day and night to create a good impression. However, I eventually worked myself to the bone. I completely wore myself out and gradually became more and more depressed. I reached the stage where I knew I needed help and so I visited my doctor. It was January 1988. I was taken into hospital the day after the visit for an indefinite period. My first thought was for my job; I didn't want to lose it and I was also extremely concerned about what other people would think. I didn't spare a thought for myself and the condition I was in; my job seemed far more important.

This was the first of two inpatient stays and one that I would care to forget. I was admitted to a psychiatric ward where the average age must have been at least 60. I was petrified and very lonely. It was my first time in hospital and my immediate thought was to go home. I was told that I couldn't. The regime which followed for the next three and a half months was extremely old-fashioned and barbaric. It proved to be useless. The aim of the treatment seemed to be a case of fattening me up and sending me home. I was weighed when I arrived and set a target weight which I had to reach before I was allowed home. A contract was then drawn up and forced upon me. Naturally I rebelled. The last thing in the world I wanted to do was eat and put on weight. To begin with I was given quite a lot of freedom but I abused it. I would cheat like mad, playing one set of staff off against the other, hiding food, pretending to swallow it but in fact secretly putting it into my napkin or the bin. I would do aerobics in the other rooms and even offer food to the other patients who were supposed to be on weight-reducing diets. Before weigh-ins I would drink lots of water until I was 'waterlogged'. However the staff eventually came wise to this as my weight dropped to six stone twelve pounds. My regime was made stricter at that point. I was confined to total bed-rest until I reached a weight of seven and a half stone.

I found this a pure hell that I just could not escape from although I still tried. I fought with the nurses but I could not get away with anything. My food was brought to me each mealtime and I was supervised all the time while I ate. I would then be observed for a further two hours after each meal to ensure that I did not make myself sick. If I needed to go to the toilet I was followed. But eventually the decision was made that I should use a commode instead. I was only allowed 15 minutes each day on my own either to have a bath in the morning or a wash at night. I had no privacy.

I remember lying on my bed tensing my muscles all day in a desperate attempt to work off any extra calories. At one point I had bruises all down the back of both legs where I used to tug at my skin to try and tighten it up. It was not long before this was noticed and the supervision was stepped up even more as a result. What really surprised and shocked me was the fact that the focus was on feeding me up to produce a change in my body, but never once did they take my mind into consideration. The way I was feeling did not seem important to them. I received very little in the way of counselling. It would take place once a week but only if I was lucky. Even then it didn't seem to do much good and I knew in my heart that I was not ready for change anyway.

I eventually made it to seven and a half stone. I will always remember saying to myself that the quicker I put the weight on the quicker I would get home. I would drink before weigh-ins and deceive the staff in any way I could. Basically I was 'eating my way out of hospital'. At the end of my stay I had not reached my target weight but I was considered healthy, physically at any rate, and so I was able to discharge myself. I continued with outpatient hospital visits on a regular basis and occasionally I was weighed. I returned to my job and life carried on. I was never comfortable with food and after a year I found myself back on the slippery slope although this time things got worse. By the summer of 1989 I was advised to attend a day hospital which was attached to yet another psychiatric ward. I agreed to go on a daily basis as an outpatient and from July until September I did so.

This time it was even easier to avoid food. Again playing one member of staff off against the other, for example telling one that the other had given me my morning snack and saying the same to the other, I was cunningly able to lose the pounds. I would also pretend to my mother that I had eaten at the hospital but while I was at the hospital I would go out for a walk at mealtimes. I truly hated myself for doing this. The thought of lying to my mother upset me greatly. I used to lie awake – unable to sleep knowing the pain I was putting her through. All she could see was her little girl fading away before her eyes.

I would love to come home from hospital at night and cook for my mother and brother and then watch them eat while I resisted the temptation. This would give me a great feeling of satisfaction. I'd bake cakes and make fudge and happily put it in the freezer or feed it to the others. I was never out of the kitchen. When I bought food for myself I would always check the calories first. I counted every single calorie I consumed. I was totally and utterly wrapped up in my dieting, my weight and image. Nothing else mattered. I still thought I was fat. My diet at this point consisted of a few mouthfuls of branflakes and maybe a few cups of black tea. Throughout the day I'd survive on diet coke. My evening meal consisted of a plate of peas, brussel sprouts or salad plus more juice to fill myself up.

The only time I really began to panic and feel frightened was a few days before my twenty-sixth birthday. I was still attending the day hospital but was eating virtually nothing. I would get up early so that I could go through the breakfast ritual of filling a bowl with branflakes, pouring on the milk and then forcing the whole lot down the sink. Now and then I would chew a few mouthfuls but I would never swallow anything, I spat them out instead. I would then leave a couple of single flakes in the bowl so that it looked as though I had eaten them all. At this point in my life everything I ate was too much. I would even think twice before licking a postage stamp for fear of any sugar coating on the gum! I would go through a similar routine with the toast. I'd make it so that the smell would rise upstairs and then would sprinkle a few crumbs on a plate and dip the knife in the marmalade. I would then either feed it to the dog or wrap it in paper and throw it away later. I didn't even chance putting it out for the birds in case it was noticed. I was aware, however, that part of me wanted people to know what I was up to because deep down I knew that things had gone further than ever before. For the first time in my life I felt scared. I was torn between two voices in my head – one saying I needed help and the other saying I could cope.

It was not too long before the doctor attached to the day hospital asked to see me. Unknown to me the staff during the day had been concerned about my health and rapid weight loss over the summer and they suggested that I come onto the ward. Knowing what I knew from my previous inpatient visit I flatly refused. However, after discussion with the doctor it was doubtful if in fact I would be allowed to have a say in the matter. The medical staff claimed that I was a danger to myself and that it would be better for me to come into hospital voluntarily rather than against my will. A lengthy discussion followed and I was assured that the regime on this particular ward would be totally different to before. The next day I was admitted.

Looking back now at my health at the time the situation was pretty severe. I was unable to sleep; I was always cold, tired, anaemic, withdrawn, frightened and depressed. I was even beginning to grow fine hair on my arms and legs. I was grateful that I did not lose any of my hair although it appeared lank and listless. For the next nine months I remained as an inpatient. A much slower yet steady care plan was drawn up. I had a lot more say in my treatment programme and received much more in the way of psychotherapy. I had regular meetings with the key worker on the ward and still had to attend the day hospital as well. Things were not easy at the start. To begin with I refused anything but a couple of mouthfuls. I was supervised during and after my meals. Food had become even more of an enemy to me and the ritualistic behaviour which accompanied it was incredible. I had to sit a certain way on my bed to eat the food. I wouldn't allow any of it to touch my lips and after every mouthful had to wipe my face. I would also eat in a set sequence – the 'safer' foods first, followed by the rest. When the food was placed in front of me I would panic so much that my breathing would quite often become so erratic that it was followed by a mild panic attack.

My weight dropped under six and a half stone which for a five foot six inches tall woman with quite a large frame was fairly serious. The pressure was put on me – bedrest was stepped up and so was the supervision. I underwent intense psychotherapy, reliving my past and in particular my father's death. This had always been a taboo subject but one which, according to the doctors, had a big part to play in my illness. I had always found it hard to show anger and my emotions but through the sessions it was hard not to. Many claimed that I was punishing myself as a result of what had happened to my father. Others thought that Anorexia could also have had a lot to do with the control I had in my life. Everything I did I had total control. In my eating I *had* to control what I ate – I had to have the perfect image. It was also suggested that as my father was overweight, and this may have been a contributory factor in his death, I couldn't let the same thing happen to me. In reality I suppose looking back it was a form of slow suicide. I wanted to see my father again and Anorexia could have been a way of achieving this goal.

Reality struck one day during a psychotherapy session when I came to realise that I wasn't going to see my father again. I remember vividly becoming hysterical, crying my eyes out. I was so angry and couldn't understand why my father had to die. I remember throwing my cup and tipping my food tray all over the floor – something that I would not have dared to do years ago. The perfect Fiona could do no wrong. Everything I did as a youngster was always right!

It is difficult to know when the exact turning point was. I remember getting a new dietitian to whom I really related. The emphasis was never on calories or target weights but how I was feeling and coping with the changes in my diet and in my body. We worked very slowly and gradually my weight increased. It was a desperately slow process but with all the support I got from her I made progress. It was slow but it was in the right direction. It is a very true saying that to starve the body you starve the mind. At this point my body was so severely undernourished it was obvious that there was no possible way my mind could think straight. Gradually as my weight increased my thinking did change for the better. I had a lot of decisions to make. Would I stay where I was or try to move on? I decided to move on a little.

Today I still struggle at seven stone but I am able to function more comfortably on a daily basis. My periods returned after a seven year gap and the best thing of all was that I got married four years ago. That has helped considerably. The focus of my life is no longer on *me, me, me,* but instead is on *us.* Life is much more fun again and my self-esteem and self-worth has increased. I feel now that I am worth more and deserve some good in my life.

My husband and I socialise a lot and we have a happy life together. I have to say to myself continually that I may be a little heavier but that I have gained so much more than just weight. I have moved away from the living hell I used to endure. I was merely existing before. All I can do now is to keep looking forward and thinking of the future. In my career as a Physical Education teacher I have come into contact with many adolescent girls who have shown signs of, or actually had, Anorexia. Due to the nature of Physical Education and my caring approach many have put their trust in me. It has given me a great feeling of satisfaction to be able to help them by passing on some of my knowledge of the illness. If anything has come out of my illness it is that hopefully my experience can be used to help others in a positive and constructive way in my profession by being able to spot the danger signs and to act upon them quickly. I hope that by doing this success-fully I can prevent these children from having to endure the dreadful suffering that I went through. To stop just one will make my suffering worthwhile.

CHAPTER 3

The Anorexic Child

'The longer I did not eat the more attention my parents
gave me and the less time they spent arguing.'

*Carla is just twelve years old. She developed Anorexia at the age of nine. At
such an age it is obviously difficult for the person to be able to examine the
psychology behind their eating problem, but Carla like most anorexics is of
above average intelligence and is extremely articulate. The illness also seems
to have forced her to grow up quickly. She has experienced the darker side of
life and lost her childhood innocence. She puts forward her story very well.
It is left to the reader to formulate the hypothesis as to why Carla became ill
although many contributory factors are obvious. Carla's story illustrates the
level of trauma children go through when they hear their parents constantly
arguing and they fear that their family will split up. Carla's illness gave her
parents something in common, something they could both focus on instead of
the problems they were experiencing in their marriage. Carla seemed very
aware of that and so her Anorexia served a useful purpose until the point
came when she was just too ill.*

I don't like eating. In fact I don't think I like food – I'm not sure really.
A lot of people ask me why I don't like to eat and that is my answer. I
have seen a lot of professionals. They always say that it is more
complicated than just not liking food but I don't think it is. Not
everyone likes food and I am one of those people.

I clearly remember the day I stopped eating. It was shortly after my
ninth birthday. My parents and I went to the cinema and then to a

restaurant for a meal. It was a nice evening until the food arrived. My mother mentioned something about my schooling. They had been talking a lot about me going to secondary school. That must have upset my Dad because then they started arguing. Dad wanted to pay for me to go to a private school but my Mum said I would get an excellent education where I was, and anyway we could not afford it. They did not ask me what I thought about it all and it was something they argued about a lot. I did not want to move to a different school. I wanted to go to the same school as all my friends. I did not like to say anything though – I didn't want them to shout at me as well.

That evening in the restaurant I was upset about their arguing and I did not want to eat. I no longer felt hungry and so I left the meal. My Dad was concerned and my Mum was a little annoyed at first but I said I had stomach ache and she was worried after that. I ate a few small pieces of chicken; the rest of the meal I left. My parents kept asking me if I was all right. They spent the rest of the evening discussing my health because they were both concerned. I was pleased that they weren't fighting any more.

When I woke up the next day I remember feeling really hungry; I couldn't wait to have breakfast. I could hear my parents downstairs, arguing. I heard my Dad saying that he was going to go away for a while. He said he could not bear being in the house any longer. I was upset. I did not want him to leave. I joined them for breakfast and hoped that I would find out what the problem was. They started arguing about money again and my Dad said my Mum was spending too much and that she should get herself a better job with more money rather than spending his all the time. I suddenly felt sick and stopped eating. Then my parents started taking notice of me and for the first time that morning they stopped arguing.

I remember feeling dizzy and my Mum said I could stay off school. My Dad came home at lunchtime to see how I was. He did not usually do that and it was nice to see him. The longer I did not eat the more attention my parents gave me and the less time they spent arguing. I felt happier because they were not so angry with each other all the time but I was worried that if I ate they would stop looking after me and would start arguing again. Since they had become concerned about me they had stopped fighting. It therefore seemed like my job to keep them together. My Dad said he worried about me. I asked him if he was going to leave. He said that he was having some problems with Mum but would stay around while I was poorly. I did feel poorly. At first I had felt very hungry but after a while that passed and I just felt sick and very, very tired. My parents looked after me very well and hardly argued at all. I was very pleased.

My teacher at school would often ask me if I was all right. I didn't always eat my dinners. I had to look pale so that my parents would know I was ill. My hands were often very cold and looked yellow. This concerned my teacher too. My friends started saying I looked thin. They often looked after me and protected me. I liked that. I liked being the smallest person in the class. It made me feel important.

I was pleased at Christmas time that my parents had not argued that much for six whole months. That was the result of me becoming ill. I had been concerned that my Dad would have left by Christmas but he was still living with us. I felt so much happier but I was still concerned that if I got well the arguing and fighting would start again. I was also worried because I was feeling worse than usual. I could not stay on my feet for long and at night I could not sleep. I had a lot of bruises on my legs and hip bones and it was painful when I sat down.

My Aunt stayed with us for a week just before I was due to return to school. She is my Mum's sister but lived in Scotland so we had not seen her for many months. She did not visit London that often. I liked her visits because she always bought presents. That year she brought lots of chocolate and sweets and I cried when she gave them to me because I knew I could not eat them. It was not just because I wanted to stay ill; it was because I felt sick after even the smallest mouthful of food. I used to eat big meals but now the sight of a plateful would upset me too much.

Aunt Janet is a nurse. She told Mum I had a serious problem. I heard them talking one morning. They had not heard me creeping down the stairs. I know now that she had told Mum that I had Anorexia, but at the time I had not understood the word properly and had not known what she was talking about. The doctor explained it to my Mum and me several days later when I was taken to see him. He said I had an eating disorder and if I continued to lose weight I would have to go into hospital. I had not been in hospital before and the idea scared me but when he weighed me I was exactly five stone and I knew that the moment I ate and put any weight on everyone would think I was getting better. I did not want that to happen because I did not want things to go back to the way they had been before. I was determined not to go above five stone and, if anything, I wanted to lose more weight.

My aunt is a very big lady. She always ate a lot when she visited us. My Mum has always worried about her size too. I think she is worried she will get as big as Aunt Janet, so she has always been on diets. There is a poster on our fridge that says 'A moment on the lips, a lifetime on the hips'. I see that every time I go into the kitchen. It always reminds me not to eat. Mum also has a chart that she got from her slimming club. If she has a good week and loses weight then she puts a gold star on it. I have my own chart in my room although I didn't let my parents see it. If I ate nothing all day, I gave myself a gold star.

Just before my tenth birthday my parents hired a nanny called Susan to look after me. I was not allowed to go to school until I was a little better and because both my parents went out to work each day Susan was hired to look after me. I did not like her. She didn't really talk to me that much. She only seemed to take notice of me when it was mealtimes but I did not eat with her because I wanted to get away from her. So I told her I wanted to eat on my own in my room. She said that was all right as long as I ate everything on my tray. I didn't of course – I hid it all in the wardrobe. I sometimes ate a piece of fruit. I knew that would not put weight on as I had read one of my Mum's diet books; there were a lot of them in her bedroom. Her scales were there too and I weighed myself after eating or drinking anything to check that my weight had not gone up. I also weighed myself at the beginning of every day while Susan was making breakfast. Shortly after she joined us I was five stone. Three weeks later I was four and a half.

I will never forget the morning before my birthday when I woke up to hear my parents arguing again. They had not argued for ages and I cried in my bed as I heard them. Then I realised they were arguing about me. Apparently my Mum had just spoken to the doctor who had said that I would probably need to go into hospital. My Dad was angry with her for not taking time off work to look after me. Then he said that I had stopped eating to be on a diet like she had been on for the last few years and that it was all her fault. I got out of bed at that point and went downstairs to see them. They stopped arguing when I came into the kitchen but I was still upset because they looked angry. I knew it was all my fault. They were arguing about me. I said I wanted to have some breakfast. I never ate breakfast and I could see that they were pleased I wanted something to eat. They looked happier and it did not look as if they were going to start arguing again.

Mum made me toast with butter and jam on it but I knew from her diet books that butter had lots of fat in it. I did not want to eat it because I did not want to get fat. I did not want to look like Aunt Janet. She must have looked awful because Mum had spent years trying not to look like that. The two pieces of toast looked really big as well. I knew I would feel sick after eating them. I looked at them on my plate but nothing would make me reach out and pick them up. I burst into tears and then I blacked out.

I was in hospital when I woke up and I had a tube sticking into my nose. My parents were both there and looked pleased when I said hello to them. I did not know where I was but soon realised because I could see nurses around me. One asked me how I felt. I said I felt tired. I also had a headache. A doctor came along and told me that I was going to spend some time in hospital. I was in the Accident and Emergency Unit but they were going to take me up to the children's ward. I asked him why and he said I needed to start eating and put weight on so that I would be healthy again. He told me I had Anorexia and I recognised the name from Aunt Janet's conversation with my Mum.

I told the doctor that I did not want to eat. I didn't want to get big and fat like Aunt Janet. I said I was all right as I was. He said that I weighed four stone five pounds and that I was very ill. He said I had collapsed unconscious at home. I then felt scared and screamed at my parents to take me home but they wouldn't. They said I had to stay and be looked after. I said I wanted to be looked after by them. I promised to eat if they took me home but still they said no. The doctor then told them to leave and so they did. I hated him from that moment onwards.

I was taken to a ward with about 11 other children in it. Some of them were playing and some were in bed asleep. I was introduced to some of the nurses but I could not remember their names and I felt too tired to look at their faces. I felt ill. I wondered if I was going to die. I didn't want to. The doctor said I would be fed through a tube until I was able to eat by myself and put weight on. I cried and cried. I wanted to be with my family. I did not want to be in hospital. I told the doctor I had to be at home. I needed to know if my parents were all right. I had to know that they were not arguing and that my dad had not left home. I was told that they could visit me as often as they wanted – that was the best the doctor could do. The tube in my nose felt uncomfortable. I could feel scratching in the back of my throat, but I decided that at least while it was there I would not have to eat.

I stayed in hospital for many months. I had to spend my tenth birthday in there. I was fed a horrible-looking liquid through a tube for the first couple of months but then I began to eat and it was not as upsetting as I had expected. Mum and Dad came to visit and they seemed quite cheerful so I did not worry too much. I liked the hospital – the nurses were nice and I made a lot of friends. Some did not stay for long but there was another girl like me who was also being tube-fed. But when I started to eat she did too. I think she had the same problem as me; she was very thin and looked ugly. Her bones stuck out through her pyjamas.

It was good to get home at the end of the summer and just visit the hospital every week. I had begun to get bored of being inside all the time when it was so nice outside. We went to the New Forest for a holiday and I learnt to horse-ride. I was only allowed to exercise for short periods each day but I looked forward to it so much and it was always worth the wait. I was starting to feel stronger; I was eating small meals and food did not seem to occupy my thoughts so much.

When we got home to London at the end of the holiday my parents told me that they had some good news. They said I would be having a new baby brother or sister at Christmas. They were very happy about it and I was too. I thought it would be nice to have a little baby to look after. I thought something like that might also stop my Dad from leaving.

That was two years ago. Baby Thomas is now one and a half years old and not so much of a baby anymore. I love him so much. He has always been a lovely baby. I love him because he made my Mum and Dad happy and stopped them from arguing. I tried very hard but after a while they started arguing about me and I had not wanted that to

/A-2011/FALL - EARTH

CI130/LECT/A-2011/FALL

Quickmail   -

✉ Compose
≣ History

to SCI
rth
ce

pping
ew of how our
the
arth system
several
nomy,
em to

Latest News   −

(No news has been posted yet)

Upcoming Events   −

There are no upcoming events

Go to calendar...

happen. I am pleased now that I got better and that I can eat. I can look after Thomas so that my Mum and Dad can look after each other.

CHAPTER 4

The Primitive Days
of Anorexia Nervosa

'I fully understand how illogical it must seem to starve
yourself to near death. But Anorexia is not a concern of logic.'

*Jean lived with the horror of Anorexia for twenty-five years. Looking back
now she sees her involvement with the illness in a much clearer light. In 1957,
when it all began for her, little was known about Anorexia Nervosa. There
were no support groups, no forms of counselling, and very little understanding
of the complex illness. As a result Jean received what she calls 'guinea-pig
treatments' which today would be considered barbaric. Her fight with
Anorexia took her near to death. It also gave her first-hand experience of
human resilience and survival. At the time her fight for, and against, food
took precedence over everything and hid her underlying problems. Now, more
than a decade after her recovery, and as a survivor of Anorexia in the early
days, Jean tells her story...*

I was 22 when Anorexia took control of my life. Neither misbehaviour
nor a teenage mood could be blamed as the cause. I had long passed
that stage. In fact I had just begun teaching and, ironically, my subject
was Domestic Science. Looking back, I believe Anorexia was my
reaction to entering the wrong career.

Like many of my contemporaries, my sister included, I was guided
in career choice by my parents, in our case, our mother. My sister
completed a secretarial course and worked as a secretary until she

married. There were no ill effects. However things were very different in my case. My mother had said: 'A Domestic Science training will always be useful, dear.' And that was that. The fact that I hated science, and ended up with 'A' levels in English and French, went unheeded. There were no career talks in those days and mistakes were made. Why I never questioned the decision or changed careers later, now seems as illogical as Anorexia itself which was my way of coping with the situation.

I had been healthy, active and very keen on sport, both at boarding school and later at grammar school. Lessons and exams presented no more problems for me than they did for my friends – except an increasing dislike for the sciences. There were other factors in my Anorexia, as is often the case, but working in a food-related environment was one fraught with defiance and desperation until the end of my career. By that time Anorexia was so entrenched, so much a habit, that it was like a drug.

The three years spent at college were highlighted for me by the English option lectures. We were allowed to choose one option subject, and four students in our year chose English. Perhaps all four of us should have read English at university, but I was the only one to develop Anorexia.

Did the science lecturer sow a seed? She was given the archaic duty of weighing and measuring us. At the third year weigh-in, she produced the wry comment: 'There is no doubt Miss Menzies, you would do better if you did not weigh so much'. She recorded in the ledger...height five foot four inches, weight nine stone ten pounds...and moved to the next student. I cringed, and I never forgot the comment or the sarcastic way in which it was delivered.

Pressures of a first teaching post are obvious, but mine were increased by poor living conditions – another factor in the Anorexia. The room booked at the only boarding house in the village, where the school was situated, already had a female occupant. Without another option I had to share. Even later, when I moved to a tiny bedsit, and then to share half a bungalow with a colleague, I wasn't happy with the conditions. My weight steadily went down. Eventually Mother made me go and see our GP, who was also a family friend. My periods had stopped, and the GP, worried about this more than the weight loss, contacted a Harley Street colleague. The specialist got me a bed in a surgical ward at a high-profile London hospital. There the nurse tried to encourage me to eat and the specialist ordered a form of beeswax jelly, in the hope of inducing my periods. Both treatments had little effect. I began disposing of the food I was given. A nurse was allocated to watch me eat, which I hated. My weight fluctuated between six, and six and a half, stone. If extra ounces appeared on the scales I carried out frantic exercises in the ward's wash-room until someone came in. I also demanded laxatives.

Despite the fact that I was in a main surgical ward, an occupational therapist was asked to teach me basket-making. The cane used needed to be damp, and wet cane sprawling across a hospital ward was not popular. I was moved to a side ward so I did not cause so much disturbance.

Then with the old-fashioned idea that a sea voyage would cure all ills, the specialist recommended a holiday abroad with my brother in Rhodesia (now Zimbabwe). I resigned from my teaching post, and took a six week passage out to Africa. Weighing about six and a half stone and alone I made the trip through the Mediterranean, down the Suez Canal and east coast of Africa to Beira. Despite the excellent food aboard ship, I ate just enough to keep my weight stable. But this was the trip of a lifetime and I was not prepared to miss anything. Tagging along with various shipmates, I went ashore each time the ship docked. Unfortunately much of the trip has been obliterated from memory – like other parts of my past – due to treatments I received later. I travelled by train from Beira to Umtali where my brother met me, and drove me to Melsetter where he was living at that time.

Africa made no difference to my Anorexia. I lost a further half stone, despite the concern shown for me by my brother and his wife. They took me sight-seeing, one trip to Victoria Falls. In between I would go for walks on my own (almost into the bush), and rode a horse from the neighbour's stables accompanied by their 'boy'. The result was acute saddle-soreness and I could hardly sit down even in a cushioned chair. My brother's wife vetoed riding altogether after examining the flaked skin and raw bone. They became very worried about my condition. I realised that concentration on what was being said was becoming difficult, because my thoughts kept straying to focus on food. I had to shake myself back to reality.

The holiday was cut short. My brother booked me a seat on the next available flight back to England. He said at the time that he didn't want Mother to blame him for my deteriorating health.

On the flight I was given VIP treatment due to my frail appearance. At the end of the journey I was the first passenger down the gangway, and was escorted by an air-hostess. No one could have shown more relief at seeing parents waiting for their daughter. She handed me over like frail cargo. I must have been gaunt but at the time it did not really register. Walking down the gangway I felt a bit weak in the legs but had put it down to stiffness from the flight. Three days later I could not get up from the chair. There seemed no power in my legs. With suspected polio I was rushed to an isolation hospital where they told me I might never walk again. After some tests the doctors realised it was starvation – my muscles had wasted.

Three weeks in an isolation ward taught me the need to keep my brain and hands occupied. I was on the verge of losing my mind. Without Mother's visits bringing me sewing, embroidery, patience cards, jigsaws – anything to keep my brain ticking over – I believe I would have drifted into unconsciousness or at least into a state of total inertia.

Learning to walk again was traumatic; there was the fear of falling, the fear of the outside world, the fear to leave hold of the garden gate and walk onto the pavement. I had two sticks and Mother's help, but it took time to regain confidence. Through her imagination in thinking out ways of combating the fear – practising pavement and road drill in the village hall a few yards down the road, using the lines marked out for badminton as guides – like a child I learnt to walk again.

Motivation came from the fact that I had a second teaching post being held open for me following an interview shortly after my return from Rhodesia. Missing the September term, and with the aid of a walking stick, I began teaching again in January. The school was a type of finishing school for students over 18, and my subjects this time were laundry-work and housewifery. A large country house several miles from the nearest town had been converted into a school, with accommodation for staff in single rooms over one of the stable blocks. At least

I had my own room, made friends with the other staff, and became interested in expanding my subjects to include project work. With no food involved I felt happier, but Anorexia and anorexic attitudes were so entrenched that I could not react differently. Despite weakness in my legs, I coped with teaching in converted stables with stone floors, and a primitive stove for heating flat irons; there were electric irons but the principal was one of the old school – the electric irons could only be used for larger articles, like the church surplices which the school handled. My weight remained between six and six and a half stone. As long as I ate enough to keep going I felt life was OK, but in reality it was not.

The next six years took me through two succeeding teaching posts and various stages of Anorexia. I worked hard and there were good comments made about my teaching methods. As a result I had no difficulty in gaining new positions. However, teaching is a giving profession and energy-wise there was little left to give. Exhaustion and utter tiredness at the end of each day brought tears. After the students had gone these uncontrollable tears would spill down my cheeks – the strain of working on low reserves was taking its toll.

The second climax came in 1965. I was teaching at a grammar school, taking 'O' and 'A' level students while studying at night to keep one step ahead. I had rented a comfortable flat and living conditions were good – but I had limited my food intake to one slice of toast for breakfast, black coffee all through the teaching day, and one egg and one tomato for supper (plus a second slice of toast on good days). Inevitably the six and a half stone got drastically reduced but I did not weigh myself at this time. It was all I could do to keep up with the work, and the pain from the piles I had developed from excessive use of laxatives.

That Christmas my parents were on holiday with my brother in Rhodesia, so instead of going home I went to stay with my sister. The train journey still sticks in my mind, in particular the sweets that saved my life – at least it seemed like that at the time. I remember feeling starved, desperate for something to see me through the journey. A young girl sitting opposite me, next to her mother who was reading, had fished out a packet of sweets from her pocket. She unwrapped one and put it in her mouth. Whether the young are more sensitive or have instincts lost in adulthood I do not know but something made her offer me one, then another – and I believe that she saved a critical situation.

My sister was concerned when she saw me. She managed to get me to eat a little more over the holiday period – at rock-bottom I was willing to comply – and she insisted I bought bread for myself regularly. Anorexia and anorexic attitudes were completely beyond my sister's comprehension. She was intelligent, competent, now married with a family, and looking back I fully understand how illogical it must seem to starve yourself to near death. But Anorexia is not a concern of logic.

After Christmas and the holiday I went back to my old habits very quickly. One night I woke with extreme stomach cramp. My landlady downstairs heard my screams, and on seeing my state called an ambulance. I was rushed to hospital with suspected appendicitis – a possible ruptured appendix. Later the hospital discovered it was starvation. I began hallucinating. They gave me Complan. I drank some and refused the rest, then later woke up in the night shouting: 'I want Complan! I want Complan!' But when it was brought I couldn't drink it. Nightmares followed and the time spent in hospital passed in a fog of semi-recognition of what was going on around me. Three sixth-form students came to visit but were difficult to place in context. This really hurt, more than the physical pain.

A friend who lived nearby fetched me from hospital and I lived with her and her family until my parents returned from Rhodesia. In the corner of their small spare bedroom there appeared an angel beckoning me to come to the other side. Hallucinations can be clear as reality at the time they are happening. I fought, saying I was not ready yet, it wasn't time. The angel gradually disappeared through the walls; my battle with death had been won. After this experience I felt forced to resign from the teaching post, and that marked the end of my career.

The following years were spent at home, an adult, once again returning to the nest. Like many mothers of anorexics, my mother was too close. She became an additional factor in the anorexic fight. She always did her best, helped and encouraged in every way she could, but we were both sensitive people. Any disturbance at mealtimes – such as the telephone, doorbell, or a chance remark – would end the meal, often not only for me but also for my mother. My father was there too but he would continue eating. He became the steady third party and without him there would have been many more upsets. However, it was my mother's imagination that helped combat the physical problems I faced – extreme cold, night cramp, and little flesh on my bones. I wore layers of extra clothes, had a baby pillow between my knees at night, and a strip of foam for the bottom of the bath. Mother would bring up a hot drink if I couldn't sleep. Sometimes things were so bad at night I would sleep in her room, and father would move into the spare room.

Most of the time we had meals in the kitchen. The kitchen table was placed so that one chair, mine, was under the kitchen mantelpiece where the original solid fuel range had been. Getting up quickly from the chair one day I knocked my head and fell unconscious. I remember nothing of what happened next. Apparently I was taken to hospital where I remained unconscious for many hours. My parents were told I might not come round at all. They waited at the hospital all night. Finally I returned to a state of semi-consciousness in which I had no understandable contact with the world around me. Mother began reading the newspaper to Father, whose poor eyesight did not allow him to read print. She was reading an article about Rhodesia. Suddenly I said 'Why doesn't anyone else talk to me about Ian Smith? I know who he is – the Prime Minister of Rhodesia'. At last I was back in the real world, but at a weight of just four stone ten pounds – it had been touch and go. Later the hospital wanted me to have a brain scan but I refused. I believed the scan might prove me insane.

In the late 1960s and 1970s there were still no definite forms of treatment for Anorexia Nervosa. In the hands of psychiatrists, and as a patient in a clinic, I now became a guinea-pig for what today would be considered antisocial, if not barbaric, treatments.

Almost on arrival at the clinic a nurse started thrusting food into my mouth. She used enough force to cut my lips and made me fear losing some teeth. My mother had not yet left the clinic at the time and she spoke to them in no uncertain terms telling them that she would not have them treating a daughter of hers in that way. Her anger caused quite a disturbance in the ward and this form of treatment was, thankfully, never repeated.

Two days later, in the early morning, I was given an injection of insulin, then left without any food. To be given insulin when you are not diabetic, then to be left without food, is an experience never to be forgotten. The ward began spinning around me – there was no vertical, no horizontal. Reality began slipping away. On the point of unconsciousness I was brought a plate piled up with sweet soggy cornflakes. With what little consciousness remained, I gobbled it down, and the world finally stabilised. There followed a large pile of toast which I also ate. The treatment had no effect on Anorexia – how could it?

For the rest of the day I ate nothing. The procedure was repeated two or three times more. After that they gave up. But where were the ethics in such a sadistic form of treatment? What were the long-term side effects? I believe it did upset the body's natural insulin balance – there are times, all these years on, when the world around me spins until I counteract it with food.

In the 1960s and early 1970s psychiatrists in general believed electroconvulsive therapy (ECT) was a suitable treatment for most mental problems. How ECT – sending a high voltage current through the brain – could help Anorexia I have no idea. As a patient in a psychiatric clinic at the time I have firsthand experience of its wide, and often incorrect, usage. I was given ECT on three occasions. I did not want the treatment, but was forced to go through with it. Again I question the ethics of enforcing such treatment on any patient. Electrodes attached to the head and a charge sent through the brain – how is this likely to benefit the anorexic? When I came round from the anaesthetic it was like nothing I have ever experienced before or since – no similarity to coming round after an operation. I was confused, disorientated, did not know who I was, where I was, what had happened in the past or what I was going to do next. Many pieces had to be put back together but some never were; some memories were lost forever. I resent this loss. If this tale had been written a decade ago, it would have been far less comprehensive. Some memories have returned, but there are still gaps. The brain is the most intricate part of our human anatomy – any interference such as ECT should only be used when no other treatment is possible. It is definitely not suitable as treatment for Anorexia.

This was also a time when tranquillizers were considered to be a suitable way of treating most mental problems. They were easy to administer, time-saving for the medical profession, and could be prescribed over long periods of time. There was not a great deal known of the damaging side effects from the drugs; patients were guinea-pigs. Some managed to get off the drugs before much damage was done and some drugs had less side-effects than others but I believe there should have been more medical knowledge before, rather than after, their use. Tranquillizers are still prescribed but, I trust, with more caution. There should be a notice on the packet – 'may damage your health' – as well as the existing caution that it is inadvisable to drive or drink alcohol when taking this drug.

I was prescribed a variety of tranquillizers starting with valium, melleril, largactil, and finally modecate – the latter being given as an injection and considered suitable for anorexics. Whether this was the correct name or whether I was not being told the exact drug used, I will never know. Certainly it was the one which had the most side-effects. The largactil came in the form of a thick, resinous, evil-smelling liquid, supposedly easier to absorb in this form. When I refused to take any more, and threw the remainder of the bottle down the sink, the smell hung around for hours – even cold water could not wash away such a smell. The modecate injection went into my arm but as this was so thin Sister found it difficult and changed to injecting it into my seat, making sitting painful again.

I was on tranquillizers from 1969 to 1981. Most of the time I felt like a zombie. It was an effort to do things, even walking upstairs to fetch a book was difficult, and I couldn't read it anyway because the print was so blurred. I lost not only will-power but confidence, independence and the normal thinking power of the brain. Everything seemed difficult, each day a basic existence to be endured somehow. On bad days I couldn't even manage to go shopping in the village, let alone a trip into town. I developed migraines, some of which were psychosomatic – like before an appointment with the psychiatrist. Both types came often, and in the case of the real migraine the pain was raging and I had to lie down in a darkened room until the worst was over. Then there were bouts of uncontrollable shaking, tears, and unwarranted exhaustion. During these years my weight was about six and a half stone. The daily battle with food was automatic, part of a way of life; no decisions were necessary. I ate the minimum, except when I got very low and would eat more – if I was in bed for a few days, perhaps. I counted calories too, allowing myself about 800–900 a day.

Towards the end of 1980 and the beginning of 1981, the will to live returned. I had been only partly living for years, in fact from the beginning of the psychiatric treatments.

It was not easy to kick the habit of Anorexia and neither was it easy to kick the tranquillizer dependency. However, as I never believed I was dependent on tranquillizers, and it was only the psychiatrist who said I could not manage without them, the kick had to come from me. He had said that I would probably need modecate for the rest of my life, ironically making the comparison to a diabetic needing insulin.

Up to this point I had accepted treatments forced on me – now I rebelled. I wanted to live. Whether the changes in attitude had any relevance to hormonal changes I do not know – I do not have enough medical knowledge to draw a definite conclusion – but during 1980 my periods started again. Having missed them for nearly 23 years it is quite amazing that they returned and just shows that, after so much abuse, the body still has the capacity to repair itself. I put on a little weight which allowed this to happen, eventually reaching seven stone. Rebellion for me meant refusing the injection. There was no gradual decrease in dosage; it was just cut dead. I missed psychiatric appointments and Sister would come out to the house, determined to give the injection. I would still refuse and after several such visits she gave up. There were no more psychiatric appointments, no more treatments. I felt a cloud lift from the horizon.

But, under the cloud, side-effects had festered. Now I had to cope with claustrophobia, agoraphobia, and more bursts of uncontrollable shaking. The difference lay in the fact that after withdrawal there could be life. It took the best part of three years before the worst was over. There were no self-help groups for people on tranquillisers in the early 1980s, at least very few, and none in my area. I struggled alone with the help of friends. I began to value friendship and felt a growing need to get back into the world, to be interested in what was going on around me. As an anorexic I had lived in my own world. During the first years, I moved in the outside world but had little real interaction with it. In the last years, I was more like a zombie from another planet.

It is doubtful whether an anorexic can be totally cured. There are bound to be relapses, perhaps in times of stress – sudden aversions to food which catch you unawares and have to be controlled and a sudden inability to eat when people are around who you think are watching, when in fact they are not.

I wasted 25 years of my life as an anorexic. I lost friends and caused my family a great deal of stress. The family plays a part in Anorexia; they are not necessarily the cause but just as you suffer with it, they suffer too. Their frustration is that there is little they can do in altering the course of the illness. Families are like spectators in the front row, too close for comfort, encouraging and applauding when they do not understand the underlying plot and silence would be more appropriate.

I had treatments forced on me which should never have been allowed in our civilised and advantaged society. Thankfully, anorexics today do not have to suffer in this way. With greater understanding of the illness and help during the early stages there is hope for the future. There is also an end to the tunnel, as I hope this tale has shown. More than a decade on, I feel richer for the experience, and hope to have proved that Anorexia Nervosa can be survived.

CHAPTER 5

Anorexic Hell

'I hope I can find the strength to begin at last to get to know
myself before the Anorexia completely destroys me.'

*Joanne is currently desperately ill. Her weight is less than four stone but Joanne
does not want to be that way. She has been able to provide us with a short
account of her long struggle. It shows how dangerous and destructive
Anorexia can be and is a message to everyone to seek help as early as possible
and to do all you can to fight the illness. It isn't just weight that you lose, but
your friends, your job, and possibly even your life.*

Confidence in myself, in becoming the person I want to be and not the
one anyone else wants me to be – this, I've discovered, is the underlying
cause of my 30 years of anorexic hell.

I was a very insecure child and clung desperately to my mother. I
became not only shy, but also scared of men. I contribute this to the
fact that my father was never at home to talk to or to be with, he always
seemed to be at work, leaving my mother to bring up the family. This
seemed to make my mother over-protective to my sister, brother and
especially to me being the youngest.

I tried to make things 'right' for my mother by being 'good.' So I
took the role of the quiet, uncomplaining one of the family, never
saying 'no' to anyone or anything, so at mealtimes I ate all that I was
given and if more was offered I accepted whether I was hungry or not.

I also felt that I had to be a perfectionist in all that I did so that my
father would be proud and notice me. (I know my parents loved me

whether I succeeded or not.) I became nervous of trying anything new in case I got things wrong. So really food became my comfort. I felt it pleased people if I never refused what was offered. When I was eating I felt I was able to fade into the background, and so not be involved with the pressures around me.

By the time I was ten years old I had become so nervous of everyone that I was afraid of going to school. This was mainly the result of having a male school teacher and the fact that my weight was causing ridicule at the time. I was not fat, just plump. Today the problem would have been diagnosed as 'School Phobia' but thirty years ago it was frowned upon and no psychological reasons were ever discussed. In order for me to have the confidence to attend school I was placed in a children's psychiatric unit in order to lose weight. One day I was given a 'calorie counter' book so I could tot up my daily intake. Bread and potatoes were taboo, although on some occasions I was given them as a test to see if I would be able to refuse them – I always did!

If I ate only an apple a day and lost more weight that week than the last then I received a lot of praise indeed. There was no mention of the fact that the body needed a certain amount of calories each day in order to survive, just to keep the body ticking over. Today my mind simply cannot accept the amount of food, and hence calories, that the healthy body needs. Since that day I can honestly say I became anorexic, and calorie counting and food phobias became my life. No one ever mentioned Anorexia to me. In fact it was not until I was 20 that it was diagnosed, during the second time I was admitted to hospital to be 'fattened up'. I am now 40 years old and the hell continues.

My life has been completely ruined by Anorexia. I have never had a real job because I have never been fit enough, and my dream of nursing has been unattainable because I can't, even now, concentrate on studying due to the lack of food which affects my thinking. I'm afraid of getting close to people and of making friends in case they call at mealtimes, or want me to go for a day out. I have no clothes apart from the ones I live in. Even children's sizes are too big. I have had no relationships, but I long for them now. Being treated by male nurses has helped me to overcome my fear of men.

However, I feel my Anorexia to be very different from other typical 'textbook' examples and I really prefer to call it a food phobia. I can see how emaciated I am and cry from frustration that I seem powerless to do anything about it. I am at present 23–24 kg (less than four stone) yet I see food as just calories and the logical side of my mind cannot override the illogical side. I yearn to have a womanly figure, to have friends, a home of my own, a job and a relationship – in other words *a life!*

In the region in which I live there is no specialised eating disorder unit or any understanding of food phobias. It was not until four years ago, out of sheer desperation, when I was holding a handful of tablets wanting to end it all, that a voice in my head decided I wanted to live. I phoned every person and every place that I could think of including hospitals outside our NHS region. I was finally accepted at an eating disorder unit, this being some 50 miles away. Unfortunately at the time my weight was under 22 kg and I was placed on a section under the Mental Health Act. I was tube-fed having been given just two days to live without it. This has also been the case several times since.

At this particular unit everyone was treated as individuals. I fully agree with this approach. Patients' needs, dietary and mentally, are respected, along with the weight gain the patient will feel comfortable with. However, I feel the underlying reason for why I am as I am today is that I was left to fester too long. I believe that if I had received treatment years ago I would have conquered Anorexia by now. But at least I am aware of its cause although there are many more questions that I frequently ask – Who am I? What is normal? What is right? How does food become a thing you need to live and not life itself? If only I knew. I am sure that I will find the answers once I develop into the person I am meant to be – the person that has never been able to develop. Everyone has their own character, personality and likes and dislikes over food. What does it matter if we cannot achieve ten out of ten all the time?

I have now been offered intensive psychotherapy at a hospital which is nearer but still out of our NHS region. The travelling, however, is just too much at the moment. My physical state is cause for concern and, until I can improve my weight, the therapy cannot begin. I am too focused on food, my capacity for complex thought has severely diminished.

I hope I can find the strength to begin at last to get to know myself before the Anorexia completely destroys me.

Joanne was hospitalised one month after writing this account. She is making slow progress.

CHAPTER 6

Anorexia: A Male Perspective

'I had become a walking encyclopaedia of nutritional and training knowledge but was using it to destroy myself.'

Simon provides a thorough account of anorexic suffering from a male perspective. As Simon has been able to use his experiences, and has qualified as a person-centred counsellor, he has considerable insight into the causes of his problems. He provides an interesting message to magazine publishers and shows that it is not only females that feel pressurised by the media to strive for the perfect figure. Simon's message to sufferers struggling to get better would be that it is possible, and he is proof of that. Anorexics possess amazing drive and self-discipline. This is capable of destroying them but can also be their saviour, as Simon discovered. He used the drive and self-discipline that had fuelled his eating disorder and channelled it into his recovery. We are all capable of doing the same. Simon now works as a volunteer postal counsellor for the Eating Disorder Association.

It is quite difficult to know where to begin because an eating disorder builds up gradually over time. I believe that the development of my eating disorder started around 1976 when I was at college training to be a teacher. Since the age of 15 I had regularly trained with weights and I developed reasonable muscles, along with a little self-confidence. I did not have many friends at the time and stayed away from parties and drinking, preferring to train at home.

I had always suffered from low self-esteem and lacked confidence, mainly because I was quite 'tubby' as a teenager, and did not feel attractive to girls. Weightlifting made me feel better about myself and I did slim down somewhat. During 1976, however, I noticed that many weight-trainers looked different to me; they had so much more muscle tone. I did not have that definition and so I started to investigate my diet. Around the same time various films were being shown containing fit and muscular actors. They made me realise that they had the sort of body I wanted. I can clearly remember the day I started my 'diet'. It was a Friday in mid-September and I had arrived back at the college for the new term. The canteen was shut and so I went into a pub in town. I ordered a cheese and egg salad. That became Day One. I did have a rough idea about dieting at the time. I had learnt a lot from reading muscle magazines. They seemed to argue that I should eat a lot of protein. However, this is where some of my problems with food started. I cut back on carbohydrates reasoning that they made you fat. Articles written about food at the time (mid-1970s) recommended cutting out starchy foods and using protein-based meals to achieve weight loss.

At first I felt wonderful and had a great sense of achievement. I could visibly see the changes that were happening to my figure. My stomach muscles, when I tensed, stuck out for the first time and I was thrilled!

After that my whole life became totally focused on training and watching my diet. I trained at the rowing club in Hereford where I had open access to the weights. I stepped up my training to six days a week as the magazines had advised. Throughout the autumn and winter of 1976 my body weight dropped from around 12 stone to nine stone six pounds at a height of five foot eight inches, medium build. My muscles all stuck out prominently when I flexed them and all my college friends gave me admiring glances. From the outside I looked good and this was reinforced by others as well as my own perceptions of what a good body was supposed to look like. But far more significant changes were taking place inside my head.

I became increasingly uptight and anxious about losing what I had achieved. This anxiety was only lessened by stepping up my training programme and cutting back further on my food intake, particularly carbohydrates. Soon the only starches I would take in were salads and a little dry bread. I was now training seven days a week. If I missed a day I would become anxious and depressed. I would sit in lectures pinching myself to feel for excess fat. I was totally obsessed, to the exclusion of my college work and friends. I would always have one eye on the clock waiting to go training after lectures.

With hindsight I can see that I was slowly sinking into an abyss of depression and despair. The more weight I lost the better I felt I looked, and the more I felt I needed to train and diet to maintain my shape. Day and night I lived with the constant anxiety that maybe one day I would revert to being 'chubby' again unless I continued to maintain this level of training and food intake. All my waking hours were concerned with food and with what I had eaten and whether it was too much or not enough. My head was constantly spinning, endlessly worrying about food. Looking back, I realise that I was developing what is commonly known as obsessive/compulsive disorder in which my anxieties about food only stopped when I went through my ritualised training and eating routines. When I trained I felt 'safe' and did not want the sessions to end because I knew that when they did I would start worrying about food again.

Throughout 1976 and 1977 my weight dropped but my muscularity increased. Around Christmas my weight had dropped to nine stone and I was concerned about going home and having to survive this 'foody' time. I told my mother that I was in hard training and could only eat protein and a few vegetables. My mother accepted this as I had been training for some six years and she therefore assumed that I knew what I was doing. I found a great sense of achievement in being able to refuse all the 'fattening' foods I was offered. It put me on a tremendous high. This elation made all the periods of intense starvation worthwhile. My weight continued to drop. I realise now that my body was cannibalising itself and that in fact the energy required for my training was being taken from my muscles. So I was lifting weights to make my muscles bigger when in reality I was losing muscle! As well as that I was gradually losing strength. I had noticed that I was not able to train as hard as I had used to.

I survived Christmas by borrowing weights from a friend. I felt all my anxiety melt away when I went to his house to collect them. It was a great relief to have them. It was as if I needed them to cope with life and without them I would be totally withdrawn and antisocial. I had noticed however that I was being more self-critical. If I had a 'bad' day then I would blow it out of all proportion as if I did not deserve to be happy and deserved to be suffering like this. I felt guilty if I experienced any feelings of happiness, no matter how small. My thoughts became extremely negative. All that was going through my head was how much more weight I had to lose. It was a nightmare. I hated my life and my body but I just could not see a way out of the mess. Life remained like this for many years until I finally decided I had to beat this incapacitating disease.

I was aware that things needed to change. I had become a walking encyclopaedia of nutritional and training knowledge but was using it to destroy myself. No one else knew what was going on. They all presumed I knew what I was doing, so it was down to me to sort it out. My eating had become more bizarre and I was unable to sleep for hunger. I had also become paranoid. I was right on the edge. Summer 1977 was a very significant time in my life. It was the end of my second year at college and I was training for two hours each day. I ate alone as I did not trust the canteen staff not to add something fattening to my food. I had no friends, just acquaintances. I never socialised. I was too tired and I also had to have my meals at set times; going out might have disrupted this routine.

It was my college geography trip to Austria that proved the turning point for me. I set off on the trip with 20 others. I had prepared my food for the journey but once we got to the hotel the food I was given was completely out of my hands. I really struggled with it. I ate bits, a few mouthfuls when I could, but I found myself becoming increasingly hungry. One day, walking through the mountains, I almost collapsed with exhaustion. My colleagues had all thought I was super fit; they had not realised that I wasn't and that there was something wrong. They were all very supportive, however, and made me eat some chocolate. This helped revive me but it also triggered a reaction in me; I started to crave sugar. During the evening I ran to the local baker and bought some cakes – I stuffed them all down, then felt dreadful and very guilty. The next few days I repeated this bingeing, and soon I was consuming mostly junk food. I just could not stop eating and dreaming of cakes, chocolate and bread. I had lost the ability to regulate my appetite and did not know when enough was enough. It was frightening.

When I returned home I decided to get a grip on my life and so tried to get back on my diet. I succeeded but only until the weekend; then I went out and binged on all the 'bad' foods again. Come Monday and I would resolve to get a grip again, and so the cycle continued, for several years in fact.

Once I left college as a qualified teacher I began working in a large comprehensive school and lived temporarily with friends. My life was still dictated by food. My weight was a little higher than previously but I still looked very thin. I could no longer look at myself in the mirror; I couldn't bear it. My stomach was my worst area – it did not look how I wanted it to look. I endured life but told no one about my problems for fear they would think I was mad. In those days very few people understood eating disorders.

My recovery was a long slow process lasting several years. Basically I cured myself due to an incident that occurred during one of the school trips I was leading. I had been particularly depressed at the time and had suddenly noticed that the children I had taken away were sitting around laughing and joking without a care in the world. I stared at them and wondered how long it had been since I last laughed like that. I then realised that I had wasted ten years of my life. These years could never be replaced. I decided there and then to use the self-discipline I knew I had to focus on getting better. I had been channelling this discipline into my diet and training. I decided to use it more positively and to get myself well.

The first thing I did was to 'de-emphasise' my food and training so it was no longer the major concern and focus of my life. I started eating at different times, but found it too traumatic at first and so just changed one meal and gradually extended it to the other two. There were plenty of set-backs and each day was a psychological battle against my safe rigidity and obsessive ritualisation of every single area of my life. I had to break down that control gradually. That made me feel scared to begin with and emotionally naked. I was exposed to life for the first time in ten years and I was completely unprepared for it. I was convinced that something dreadful was going to happen to me. The fact that it didn't did not help matters; I still waited. At times it all got too much and I would go home and lock myself away from the world. I needed a break; I needed to be alone and do my own things. I still worried about food dreadfully, worried that the local shop would run out of the foods I needed, or that their calorific value would be changed without me realising. My recovery was a clear case of two steps forward and one step back for many years, but I was making progress. I slowly disposed of some of my ritualistic behaviour. The fact that nothing traumatic occurred as a result lessened my anxiety considerably.

One activity that helped me greatly during this time was playing the guitar. I wrote many songs and became quite an expert guitar player. I began to notice that people admired certain things about me. I expect that that had always been the case but previously I had been so wrapped up in the issue of my food and weight that I had not noticed.

I never thought about seeking professional help for my eating disorder. I think, looking back, that the reason for this was the fact that in the 1970s and early 1980s there was not the extensive knowledge that there is today. I also felt ashamed of suffering from what I thought was a 'silly' disease. If I had been openly questioned about it I expect I would have denied having a problem for fear of being labelled a freak.

I think my recovery took such a long time because by giving up my eating disorder I lost so much more as well – my 'safe' world of food and weight, the high I felt at being able to refuse food and the sense of power this gave me. However I *have* recovered and I believe the reason for this to be some kind of inner strength that was trying to bring me back to some level of normality, coupled with the fact that I was in my mid-twenties with no friends and a frame of mind that was dependent on my ritualised lifestyle. I also remember, when I was ill, having to do everything in a certain way. Life became impractical and I think in a way this helped to change things. I just could not continue living like that. I would like to think that the drive and self-discipline that I had found to 'fuel' my eating disorder was now channelled into my recovery.

To be fit and lean was, in the late 1970s, as it is now, although more so, the way to be. Men are increasingly concerned about their image and appearance. The result has been a large increase in male Anorexia.

Today I consider myself fully recovered. Anorexia has left its mark though; I am very knowledgeable about food and exercise. I am a qualified personal trainer and fitness coach. The big difference is that although diet and exercise is still very prominent in my life, it occupies some of me, but not all. I enjoy eating and I enjoy training, but now they enhance my life, not hinder it.

I have thought a lot about why I developed an obsession with food and weight and I have come to the conclusion that, to begin with, I am obsessive/compulsive by nature. I do have a tendency to become obsessive about things. When I was learning to drive I became very interested in cars, and became fanatically involved in repairing them. I started to develop the unhealthy obsessive attitude to cars that I later extended to food. Now I have many interests but am aware of not going 'overboard' on any one of them. Second, I believe that the dieting I began at the age of 18 acted as a trigger to a whole host of feelings, anxieties and inadequacies that I felt about myself. These feelings were, I believe, a reaction to my parents. Both of them believed in the concept of a 'happy home' where no one talked, except about superficial things. I grew up thinking that you were not allowed to talk about anything that was not good. I can also remember not being allowed to help my father with certain things about the house as I would probably get it wrong. I grew up fearing 'getting things wrong.' This of course inhibited my social development. I grew up being told not to do 'this' or 'that'.

Even to this day I still lack confidence in some areas of life, particularly in relation to close relationships where I still find it difficult to express emotions such as anger. I was never allowed to express this emotion at home and so I internalised it and later expressed it as an attack on myself in the form of an eating disorder. My recovery took so long because the eating disorder gave me a sense of control in my life for the first time. It was hard to give that up. I needed something to replace it with, to fill the void. To realise that I was important as a person was something that I found very hard to accept. As I struggled to find and develop other interests and mix with people I had not seen for years, I gradually found that I could accept the person I saw in the mirror.

I believe my eating disorder was an accident waiting to happen. To some extent I blame the images of what a male body should look like for compounding the problem, the body-building magazines for bombarding me with muscular images and faulty dietary advice. But I know that for me food was a vehicle for all my inadequacies, and if it hadn't been food it would have been something else. Looking back I bitterly regret the effort and time that went into my obsessive/compulsive disorder. Had I put that effort into other things I could have achieved other, more meaningful endeavours.

I now live life to the full. I am a qualified 'person-centred counsellor' and so I have been able to put my experiences to good use. I work voluntarily for the Eating Disorders Association as a postal contact. Unfortunately I seem to be counselling more male anorexics than ever before. I hope I am able to offer them the specialist support that I should have asked for myself. I hope I am able to make all sufferers realise that food is not their problem, that it is just a symptom of more serious underlying issues. It is those issues that need to be dealt with effectively before a full recovery can be made. It's difficult but, as I have shown, possible.

CHAPTER 7

Starving out of Shame

'I did not realise the extent to which I was hurting the people I love.'

Few anorexics are actually overweight when they fall ill. Sara's case was different. In the beginning it was the lack of sensitivity on the part of her family doctor in response to the issue of weight that gave Sara the drive and determination to start on the road to weight loss. The strength of this determination brought her to the brink of death as she continued to lose weight when she had reached a healthier weight. Dieting gone wrong... or is it? Sara's case highlights many issues including the need for more sensitive handling of weight issues, the old-fashioned belief that Anorexia is a 'slimming disease' and the addictive nature of the illness.

Looking back I first became aware that I had a weight problem when I went with my mother to see our family doctor. The appointment had been made for my mother. I had just tagged along as well. However the doctor seemed to deal with her problem very quickly and I was surprised when he then turned to me and said, 'You seem to have a problem of your own'. At first I did not understand what he meant but he then went on to say, 'You're very overweight for your height aren't you?' I was 15 years old at the time and five foot four inches. He made me stand on the scales and they showed my weight to be ten and a half stone. He then went on to give me a diet sheet and some slimming pills. He instructed me to try them for a month and see how I got on.

When I left the surgery with my mother I just could not believe the scene that had just occurred. My main thoughts were that if a doctor thought I was fat and had actually said so to my face then it must be very serious indeed. His words made me determined to lose weight. I made a promise to myself that day that I would be slimmer when I next saw him. I did not want to be overweight and I did not want to go through the humiliation of being told I was again.

My mother went out of her way to help me and I appreciated this. She was aware of how much the doctor had upset me and she did not want to see me that way. But I didn't need that much support really because I somehow discovered this incredible will-power that I had not known existed in me. I used that to lose weight. It seemed to fall off me at first but after a while the process slowed down considerably. I had reached eight and a half stone by that time and everyone I knew was commenting on how much better I looked.

Food was always on my mind. My main focus in life had become my weight loss. I was very involved in food preparation at home. I often made the meals and then made other people eat them. I also noticed however that if I was hurt or upset about something I would take it out on myself and not eat. That was where I channelled my anger. Food had become a weapon to use against myself, and dieting had made me discover its powers. My weight continued to drop; I was eating very little now. The pleasure at being able to last all day without eating and seeing the scales go down was tremendous and it was a feeling I did not want to lose. I was soon a stone lighter weighing in at seven-and-a-half stone. But along with the weight I was losing my energy. I could feel myself getting weaker, particularly at the end of a day's work without food.

The turning point, if you could call it that, came one day when I was walking to work. For the first time in my life I fainted. The nurse in the store made me go to see my own doctor. It was then that he discovered that I was now down to six and a half stone. Without hesitation he admitted me into hospital. I had never been in hospital before and so it was all very new and very scary. I certainly did not want to be there and was convinced that I could control my food and my weight myself. I could not understand what all the fuss was about. Unfortunately I did not co-operate very well. I did not eat the food the doctors gave me. There were certain foods I felt I could eat, things like fruit and vegetables – these were 'safe' foods – and certain foods I couldn't, usually the fatty, sugary ones. As usual my mother was great and brought in food that I could eat and would eat. This disease turns you into such a selfish person; I had no idea of the torment I was causing her. I didn't realise the extent to which I was hurting the people I love.

After three days I discharged myself and went home. I felt happy there and spent a lot of time looking after my parents, cooking them meals and doing the housework. My moods varied considerably, usually with fluctuations in my weight. If my weight went up I was miserable and if it went down I was happy. I was very unpredictable and, I expect, difficult to live with at times.

It was not long before I set about losing more weight. This time it all became a lot more serious. My weight went down to four and a half stone and I was taken into hospital again. I was near to death and that frightened me. This time I co-operated, though I hated every single mouthful of food. I eventually went home weighing six and a half stone. I felt like a huge bull and food felt so uncomfortable in my stomach that it was unbearable at times. It took me a long time to get used to it. Allowing myself to put weight on was the most awful time and it depressed me immensely. By the end I must admit I couldn't cope at all and had to look for help. The doctors had tried; my family had tried; my mother in particular had done everything she could to help. It was now ten years on from that near fatal day when my doctor had handed me the slimming pills and diet sheet. I had tried to control it myself for all that time and couldn't continue with this 'half life'.

Eventually I turned to religion and found comfort and support in that. My family don't believe in God but for me turning to the Church brought me a whole new way of life and helped me to relax for the first time. For the first time in many years I am now able to eat properly every day and I enjoy every meal. My belief in God has also allowed me to look back over all that I had gone through without bitterness or regret.

The old fashioned view of Anorexia is that it is 'a diet gone wrong'. This is where it got the name 'the slimming disease'. For me this was not a diet gone wrong. I had needed to lose a little weight but it is obvious to me that I had problems and issues I needed to deal with and that dieting had provided me with something to focus on other than these problems. Food had become an issue because I was controlling it on my doctor's instructions as part of my diet, and I had found that I gained a lot more than a slimmer figure; I also gained the control in life and the sense of achievement that I had desperately needed.

Anorexia can be addictive to an extent. You get addicted to the 'fasting high' and the regular weight loss but it is a horrible illness. I don't believe that people become seriously underweight as a result of Anorexia in order to feel slim and look good, because anorexics don't look good and they never feel slim. It feels to me as if there is much more to it than that, and in many ways anorexics become trapped in the illness. We constantly torment ourselves, part of us wanting to eat, part of us wanting to starve. At very low weights you lose all logic and the Anorexia takes over completely. It's like a disease that spreads until it completely consumes every part of you. I believe people become anorexic for two main reasons. First, they gain something from being ill – the control and focus that they need. Then there is the addictive side, followed by the mental turmoil that is so difficult to break out of no matter how desperately you want to.

Why did I become anorexic? It is a question I do not wish to think about. It is all just too painful. I would not want to relive it by writing it down, but the message I do want to give is that people can get better, and I am evidence of that.

CHAPTER 8

Addicted to Food

'I used to manipulate my family to ensure that I had sufficient time and freedom to continue my horrendous way of life.'

Anne's story tells of the difficulties that children growing up in a dysfunctional home environment are often faced with. In Anne's case the main cause of these difficulties was the behaviour of her alcoholic father. For Anne, developing an eating disorder was the only way she felt she could gain some control over her life, and that included her family. For a while she was able to shift the focus of her family's attentions onto herself rather than her father, but it did not last forever. Anne's story also tells of the fine line between Anorexia and Bulimia, with Anne eventually becoming identified as a 'bingeing anorexic.' The physical problems that Anne now endures as a result of many years of suffering will hopefully prevent others travelling down the same path that she did. With that aim in mind Anne presents her story.

My greatest wish at present is to be able to refer to myself as a recovered or recovering anorexic. The number of years I have suffered from an eating disorder now outnumber the years of non-suffering. I now, reluctantly, accept that food will always be a problem for me although the degree of suffering will hopefully subside.

I am 33 years old and first fell victim to Anorexia at the age of 15. This being some 18 years ago, eating disorders were not high-profile, and while they are often referred to as being 'fashionable' nowadays, in the mid- to late-seventies they were relatively unheard of.

I can clearly remember the day I stopped eating normally. It was the day before my sister's wedding and I was convinced that I was so fat that I would ruin her day. In reality I was about a stone overweight for my height, but taking into account my age, I probably could have lost that naturally. With hindsight, I now recognise that the reason I decided to give up normal eating had very little to do with trying to lose weight and had more to do with deep-rooted family problems.

My father is an alcoholic. That had a devastating effect on family life and especially on me. When I reached puberty, my father rejected me completely, and I think that regardless of all the awful experiences that I have had as a result of his addiction, that had the most lasting effect. At the age of 15, when the Anorexia started, his behaviour towards the entire family, including my mother, brother and myself, had worsened. My parent's marriage was disintegrating. My sister was marrying and leaving home. I truly believed that my family was breaking up completely. I also believed, as is the case for many anorexics, that I was to blame, although there was no reason to take this blame out on myself.

As the Anorexia took a grip, I pushed myself harder and harder at school. I had always been classed as a high achiever academically and passed my exams with excellent results. This was still not enough, however. The only sense of achievement I felt I really had was in controlling my eating and thereby, to a degree, controlling my family. Suddenly all their focus was on me as my weight dropped from nine stone four pounds to five stone seven pounds. At this stage, at the age of 16, I was taken to the family doctor. His suggestion that I 'go home and eat properly' was of no help whatsoever. I continued at that weight for over two years. Then I realised that an easier way to control my weight was to eat what I wanted and purge afterwards, so that is what I did. My weight rose to a more acceptable six stone four pounds. I have never heard of this form of weight control before and thought I had discovered something new. I had in fact become bulimic.

Inevitably my mother recognised that there was still a problem and we discovered a private centre for eating disorders where I was seen by a counsellor for one hour each week. This suited me well because it allowed me free time away from the watchful eye of my mother to shop for the next binge. This is one example of how manipulative and cunning I became; I was actually using the time with the counsellor to plan to binge food I would buy on the way home. I began to learn every possible way that enabled me to continue the pattern of shopping, bingeing and purging. Throughout all this my father's behaviour worsened and he became abusive, both physically and verbally. The focus began to shift from my problem to my father's which allowed me more freedom to continue the Bulimia.

From the age of 17 to the age of 25, I continually changed jobs, always for the better, but always to 'make a fresh start'. Each new job would change the routine and the ritualistic behaviour – so I thought. In reality, however, I merely changed the job to suit the routine.

My brother left home during this time, leaving only my parents and myself. Also during this time, I tried numerous sources of help for my eating disorder, as by this stage, they were higher-profile and self-help groups were being set up. I attended the local psychiatric hospital and, through the same hospital, a centre specialising in eating disorders. I attended all their self-help groups and took part in their research, often finding this detrimental to my health as in the case of a drug study, but still saw no signs of recovery. I participated in any local self-help groups that became known to me and, whilst building up a great deal of knowledge of eating disorders and making many friends, this was all to no avail.

So here I am at the age of 33 still bingeing and purging. I am now self-employed, having returned to full-time education at the age of 26 to study for a business degree and graduating with honours. I am living with my partner who obviously realises there is a problem around food but who has no idea of the severity of the problem. I now manipulate him in the same way I used to manipulate my family to ensure that I have sufficient time and freedom to continue my horrendous way of life. I do not believe that there is anything a fellow eating disorder sufferer could confide in me about their behaviour that would shock me. If I have not done it all, I am sure that, through the various forms of treatment I have tried, I have heard of it. I wish I hadn't.

How has this affected my life generally? My social life is non-existent. I have managed to maintain most of my long-term friendships but do not socialise with my friends in a normal fashion. Most of my relationships are by telephone with the occasional meeting.

Healthwise, for my age, I think I have experienced more than most. My kidneys almost failed when I was 18 due to the fact that I did not recognise the sensation of thirst. I have lost almost all my teeth due to the acid produced whilst vomiting. I have the onset of osteoporosis, which was discovered during a body scan when I was participating in research for the psychiatric hospital. I have permanently swollen glands and have often suffered from blocked salivary glands. I could go on, but if the thought of any of these problems commonly caused by an eating disorder deters a possible future sufferer, writing this will have been worthwhile.

So where am I now? At present I am six stone at a height of five foot three inches. I binge and purge once a day and the medical profession term me a 'bingeing anorexic', not that terms and labels such as these help anyone. I continually set myself goals of when I will improve or recover but these regularly pass with no real effort being made. I would certainly class much of my behaviour now as compulsive and ritualistic and whilst much of the work into eating disorders tries to identify triggers, I know that a lot of my problems occur through habit in the same way as alcoholism or drug addiction. I can only hope that one day I can say I am a recovered or recovering anorexic but now all I can say is that I honestly feel I am addicted to food.

CHAPTER 9

From Simple Dieting to
Chronic Anorexia

'It crept up on me silently and relentlessly, eventually becoming the
driving force behind my whole existence.'

*Victoria's story not only shows that people can recover from Anorexia and
go on to lead fulfilling lives, but that, with support, this can be achieved
without a hospital admission. Victoria was fortunate in having a very caring
and understanding family, and also a very patient boyfriend who stuck by her
through the worst stages of her illness, where many others would not have
bothered.*

*In her story Victoria speaks of vanity, and that she had always been conscious
of her appearance. This, perhaps, was what caused her to start questioning
her diet and her weight. Other factors might also have played a part, including
major events in her life such as her father's death, but it appears that concern
for her appearance sparked off the dieting. This dieting then led to Anorexia.
This shows quite clearly just how 'addictive' weight loss can be and how, so
easily, a simple diet can produce disastrous results as Anorexia takes over.
This is a message to everyone that Anorexia is a very powerful and devastating
illness – it takes over your life, it changes your personality, and it can kill.*

I guess the most important factor in my story is that I am vain. I'm not
particularly proud of it but it's true – and at least I own up to it! Perhaps
that is what started my illness. Perhaps the theory put forward by my
psychiatrist, many months later, is correct, that Anorexia was triggered

by the death of my father and my marriage in the same year. I will never know. All I do know is that it crept up on me silently and relentlessly, eventually becoming the driving force behind my whole existence.

During the early seventies I won various local beauty competitions and spent a year or so modelling, all of which made me even more aware of my appearance and also my weight. It was the New Year of 1975 and like many people I had gained a few pounds over the Christmas period. I decided they had to be shed. I remember it was a bitterly cold January that year but the weather did not deter me from jogging around my local neighbourhood each day after work. However, I had never been a great fan of physical exercise and so my enthusiasm for this ritual soon waned. I decided that a much more agreeable course of action would be to study what I was eating.

Like many victims of Anorexia I spent a great deal of my money on 'textbooks', namely slimming magazines, calorie-counting guides, 'get thin quick' aids, in fact any publication that even remotely touched on dieting. To put the whole issue into context I am five foot four inches and at that time weighed just over nine stones. It could have been argued that my problem was hardly worth bothering about!

With my new-found knowledge of what to eat and what not to eat my weight started to drop. I was thrilled. My average weight during my life had been between eight and nine stone and getting below that magic eight stone figure gave me enormous pleasure. I felt elegant, attractive and most importantly bony. I suddenly discovered that I had always wanted to be bony! Fuelling my illness (and my misguided vanity), my family and friends started to comment on how 'thin' I was becoming. Excellent! My diet was working!

I felt very fortunate at that time in my life to be living alone. No one was monitoring what I ate (or rather did not eat), how many hours I spent engrossed in the calorie guides or how much my social life had collapsed. I religiously avoided all social events. Spending time with other people invariably meant eating and drinking with them, and besides, seeing people eat disgusted me. It was such a revolting and self-indulgent habit! On the rare occasions when I could not avoid such gatherings, anything up to six laxative tablets were taken before going to bed, followed by a painful night and the desired result next morning. With hindsight the laxative abuse was probably the most dangerous part of my illness; any additional food over and above what had become my routine intake was attacked by laxatives.

By this point in the illness 'routine intake' was no more than 400 calories a day. This consisted of a (very) small portion of bran cereal, no sugar and watery powdered milk for breakfast, an apple for lunch followed by another apple, and one low fat yogurt for supper. In order to stave off the constant hunger pangs I drank black coffee and 'one calorie' cola constantly. My weight was now dropping rapidly and I was delighted with the way I looked and the comments I was receiving from everyone I came into contact with.

I gave no consideration whatsoever to exactly where my mission was headed; I had no 'goal' weight that I had set for myself – I never even thought about it. My whole aim in life was to be thinner than I was the day before. As I got smaller so did my clothes size, a standard size 12 went to a 10 and then to an 8. What joy being a size 8 was to me – no one else in my circle had that claim to fame! Although I had always been careful about my appearance I now became obsessive; my make-up, hair, nails and clothes had to be perfect. You see, I felt so attractive! So elegant and fragile with such amazing hip and cheek-bones!

By this time I had dropped below seven stone and things slowly started to become unpleasant. The hunger was terrible; it was with me 24 hours a day. I was on a 'fasting high' and had dreadful trouble sleeping. When I did sleep I constantly dreamt about food and had terrifying nightmares about eating high-calorie goodies. My periods stopped. The constant stream of comments about my weight loss infuriated me. The lying and deception started.

Six stone came and went and concerns over my health started creeping into my mind. The lack of sleep was wearing me down; I was constantly tired and also very, very hungry. People were beginning to invade my privacy regularly with their stupid questions, observations and advice, and I noticed that my reactions to them were becoming more and more aggressive. Sitting in the bath was becoming painful as my pelvis and spine jarred against the porcelain.

One vivid memory that I have of this time is a visit from my mother. She called over to see me and brought with her (not altogether innocently, I suspect) a family-size bar of my favourite chocolate. I was horrified that such a disgusting item had been brought into my home so I promptly threw it across the room and ordered her to get it out of my sight. My game had started to lose its appeal. I actually admitted, to myself, that perhaps I was going mad. I was scared. As I hovered towards the five stone marker my front teeth started to feel loose. That was it – I realised I was in trouble and suddenly became aware of the fact that unless I got help I would die. I was terrified and spent a long, unforgettable night sobbing with anguish at the prospect of having to eat real food again or face a certain death. What a choice I had to make…what was I going to do?

Unbeknownst to me, as I became more and more skeletal, various things were going on behind the scenes. I had been receiving medication from my GP for the sleepless nights, being very careful to wear heavy clothing and fill my pockets with coins when I went to see him, just in case he decided to weigh me. He did from time to time of course, and any mention of my weight going down was met with cool, well-rehearsed lies, and hidden fury that he was questioning my weight. My mother had been to see him – so I learnt much later – pleading with him not to let me die. He quite naturally pointed out to her that until I admitted that there was a problem nothing could be done, at least not yet.

I had started a new relationship during the course of my illness. My boyfriend realised I was thin but, as would be true of most men, did not think anymore of it. Then I made the mistake of meeting his parents! Apparently his mother was horrified at my appearance, causing him to think more deeply about various traits of mine that gradually brought them both to the conclusion that all was not well – least of all me!

Much later, when I had recovered, he reminded me about the first time I had invited him home for a meal. I couldn't remember the facts but the poor chap claimed he was served up salad, with no potatoes, no bread, no dessert, no cheese and biscuits, no nothing! He went home that evening and raided his fridge as he was starving! It also dawned on him that perhaps it was odd that someone my size *always* drank slimline tonics when we were out and never had crisps in the pub or chocolates at the cinema. Yes, perhaps his mum was right, maybe I *was* rather odd. He resolved to find out more.

All this with my mother, the GP and my boyfriend had been going on at the same time as I was waking up to the fact that I had major problems. Ironically I was a Samaritan during this period of my life (a case of 'physician heal thyself'?) and it was to one of my colleagues in the local branch that I turned. The day after the dreadful night I had spent sobbing about the dilemma I was in, I went to see him and poured out the whole sorry tale. Of course he knew. In fact everyone who knew me knew. At long last I had admitted it, and desperately wanted help. My Samaritan friend was delighted, bless him, and we both cried. I wanted to get better but I didn't quite know where to start.

I really can't recall the precise order of the events that followed – it all happened so quickly. I saw my GP who urgently referred me to a psychiatrist. I unburdened myself to my mother and boyfriend, both of whom were wonderful along with all my friends (well, the ones I had left). They all rallied round. I was given two months off work. The psychiatrist told me that I looked like a 'bicycle frame', warning me that unless I gained some weight within the next six weeks he was going to have me admitted to a local secure unit. My boyfriend emptied my flat of laxatives and intimated that unless I sorted myself out he was off! This all sounds heartless and cruel, I know, but it worked. Perhaps I am the type of person who responds well to threats.

I will never forget being faced with my 'first' Belgian bun – I just sat staring at it for ages with tears rolling down my cheeks, knowing that somehow I had to summon the will to eat it. Sounds ridiculous I know, but, I suspect, quite typical of anorexics. Slowly but surely I gained weight. My periods returned – I remember the euphoria from all concerned at this event! My teeth stayed where they were and I kicked the laxative habit. My weight increased, within a period of six months, to a respectable eight stone, and I got married.

Twenty years have come and gone since then. I am now fit, healthy and still eight stone. My family and friends maintain that I am left with an 'anorexic brain'. I can understand what they mean – I am very careful to avoid any clothes that make me look 'fat', for example pleated skirts or baggy trousers, and my weight is never allowed to creep up or down more than half a stone. My defence of this strange habit is that at least I have set myself a lower boundary as well as an upper one! Food is not an issue in my life anymore. I am fortunate that I don't gain weight easily, probably helped by the fact that I became a vegetarian nearly a decade ago. I had a worrying challenge to contend with three years ago when I had to have a hysterectomy, a procedure that is renowned for causing weight gain. With a great deal of care and consideration over my diet I managed to *lose* weight (but only a few pounds!) However, I do admit to eating a lot of junk food and could be described as a 'chocoholic', much to the envy of my friends. They are all waiting for me to suffer from middle age spread...dream on folks, not me!

CHAPTER 10

The Physical Consequences of a Mental Illness

'Sadly Anorexia has left me feeling more secure with possessions than
with people; you know that possessions cannot hurt you,
but people can.'

*Alison's account clearly shows how severely Anorexia Nervosa can damage
a sufferer's physical health. Some can end up severely disabled with problems
such as osteoporosis and other bone and joint complaints and the physical
symptoms do not end there, as Alison's story shows...*

I find it very hard to write this. Anorexia has been a part of me since I
was 12 years old and has affected the course of my life ever since. At
one time I thought Anorexia was my friend – something I could control
and take refuge in, something that caused my mother, at least, to take
an interest in me. Now Anorexia is my enemy, contributing to my
disability, leaving me with osteoporosis in my hips, back pain, painful
joints and exacerbating an existing hereditary bowel disorder through
my abuse of laxatives.

As I said, my problems started around the age of 12. Until then I
had always been plump and had worn glasses since I was about eight
or nine. I was teased because of my size but until then I had not really
let it bother me. We had a children's doctor who gave us a check-up
each year on our birthday. He used to measure our body fat. His name
was Dr. Browne and on my twelfth birthday he told my mother I was
overweight and needed to diet. I then started to become aware of my

body size, especially as my periods had already started and I was starting to fill out and develop hips and breasts. I remember putting loads of books on my stomach when I was in bed in the hope of flattening it – but the next morning it was always the same.

I cannot remember purposely cutting down on food, but I developed a great interest in vegetarianism. It was around the same time that I became very conscious of my schoolwork and began striving to be the best. I felt that my father, who had always ignored me because I was not a boy, would pay me attention if I achieved high marks. I passed my Eleven Plus to attend a top Catholic grammar school in Bristol.

I had had a very sheltered life and had been taught little at school about sex education. One day I went to meet my mother at work; she helped run a dry cleaning business. When I pushed open the door of her office it was pushed shut in my face. I had a glimpse of my mother in there; she was with the boss's husband. I was only 13 years old at the time. I did not realise what was going on but I felt dirty at having witnessed whatever it was. After that experience I became my mother's confidant. She revealed her affair with the boss's husband and her dislike of my father, who was 16 years older than her, because of his meanness, selfishness and drunkenness. Not long after that she discovered she was pregnant. She told my father it was his, but to me she told the truth – it belonged to Matthew, her boss's husband.

In a way I was happy she was pregnant. I looked forward to the brother or sister I was to gain. My mother hated the thought of being found out, so when she was six months pregnant she carried a wardrobe down four flights of stairs. She got what she wanted; she lost the baby. It was a little boy. I was devastated.

My Mum said that my father hardly gave any money to keep me at school so she had to get a job. She started going out to work leaving me in the position of having to act as a mother to my father and brother. I had to be understanding to my mother's situation without really being old enough to know what was happening. I felt I had lost my innocence and my childhood; I felt older but not wiser. I felt I had to be the mother figure. I did not want this.

I think this was the start of my Anorexia. I looked at myself and felt I wanted to be a child without these adult responsibilities. I walked to school and back each day, a journey of six miles. I started eating an apple and yogurt for lunch and nothing else. With my mother back at work I was expected to do the housework and the cooking. I loved cookery and would look at cookery books then create really fattening dishes. In the meantime I was constantly striving to be the top of my class and also to lose weight. At that time I was 14 years old and weighed about eight stone at a height of five foot four inches. I was introduced to a boy called Paul. He was tall, blond and aged 16. His father worked in Africa but he had returned to England to attend an English school. He would return to Nigeria for a few months of the year. To me Paul was perfect and I fell madly in love.

I continued to lose weight and would write to Paul when he was away. He returned to England for good when I was 15 and a half. He attended the local Roman Catholic boys school. We talked about getting engaged. But I knew nothing about sex and when he went to touch me I went to pieces. We eventually split up because he could not understand what was wrong with me.

I retreated into Anorexia and began abusing laxatives. I was eating three apples a day; I was top of my class in everything at school; I was cooking fattening meals for my family and I weighed about seven stone. I went to America to see my half sister. The attention I received over there and the popularity of Twiggy and the mini-skirt spurred me on to lose more weight. By the time I was 17 years old I was six stone and five foot six inches tall. At the time I felt great – full of life and in control of everything. I was living in a world of my own. Anorexia was my friend and sheltered me from my father's coldness and drunkenness, away from my brother's delinquency and away from my mother's cosy confessions about the boss's husband.

Unfortunately for me, my mother had actually begun to notice how thin I was becoming. The school was writing to her about their concern about my diet and the fact that I ate very little at lunchtime. My mother contacted my doctor and they arranged for me to be admitted into hospital. Hospitalisation was one of the worst experiences of my life. No one there knew how to handle Anorexia and I was with manic depressives, victims of child sex abuse, alcoholics etc. I was also one of the youngest there. They put me on a high-calorie diet and large doses of largactil. I spent my life in a semi-drugged state and was released as soon as I reached seven and a half stone. Needless to say, I lost all the weight and more and ended up totally confused at a weight of five and a half stone. I sat my 'A' Levels but did not get the grades I had hoped for. I felt an absolute failure. I spent all my time in the privacy of my room away from the hassle of relationships, listening to music. I hated my family; I just wanted my Anorexia.

I managed to go off to college but found it difficult to cope properly with 'normal' people living their 'normal' lives. I returned home weighing just over five stone and was immediately admitted to hospital again. However I could not cope with the force feeding and so I ran away to London, where, after working for a top fashion store, I found a job as a house model. There I was accepted for what I was even though I was a lot thinner than the other models. Being away from home allowed me to think more about my family and my relationship with them in a more objective way. I was now twenty years old and I felt I was coping with life.

I returned to Bristol in time for my twenty-first birthday. I lived at home until I was twenty-six and then decided I was going to move out and start my own life elsewhere. I could no longer cope with being my mother's counsellor and had no feelings for my father or brother.

Finding my own place definitely marked a turning point for me. I was working for the local government and putting on weight. I was five foot eight inches but made sure I did not go over seven and a half stone. However the Anorexia would always prevent me from forming proper relationships with men. I lost my virginity to a married man at the age of 27, and continued to have a series of relationships with men until the age of about 30. I felt that by at least doing that I did not have to commit myself to the relationship. However this ended up causing me to make a disastrous marriage to a man eight years younger than me while on the rebound from a relationship with a married man with whom I had fallen deeply in love.

My first husband was violent and a heavy drinker. I had 13 miscarriages – some caused by his violence towards me – but I was determined that the marriage would succeed. By 1983, when we had been married two years and had a son, my husband had walked out of my life.

My Anorexia had left me striving for perfection in every area of my life. My marriage had failed and so I felt totally let down. I then began to become more aware of my bowel disorder and realised that it had been made so much worse by my laxative abuse. I was living in South Wales at the time and felt I really had to grow up quickly and look after my baby son. It was very hard.

In 1986, I met my second husband. I still strive for perfection but I am now realising that it can affect my family's life as badly as it affects mine. Unfortunately my second son has Attention Deficit Disorder and my youngest son is autistic. As a result of my Anorexia and an accident at work I am now registered as disabled. So there is a lot to cope with.

Anorexia has been a friend to me but it has also been an enemy. It is like being an alcoholic. With alcoholism, if you have this problem you can no longer drink, even a mouthful. With Anorexia you have to keep away from the scales and one missed meal can lead to a never-ending downward spiral of weight loss. I am aware now that anorexics see themselves very differently from how other people see them, and that even when recovered they will always be left with that drive for perfection. This is often detrimental to their relationships with people close to them and who love them.

Sadly Anorexia has left me feeling more secure with possessions than with people; you know that possessions cannot hurt you, but people can.

CHAPTER 11

The Alcoholic Parent

'My thoughts, feelings and attitude towards myself and towards life seemed too deeply entrenched to change, and so I decided to alter drastically my physical state instead.'

Barbara, and her family, suffered dreadful physical and mental abuse at the hands of her alcoholic father. She married at the age of 17 to escape the horror of home life but by that point was too 'emotionally crippled' to cope with life in any normal manner. Her search for happiness and the love she had missed took her through several disastrous marriages. Her desperation to gain some stability, control and a sense of achievement in her life took Barbara into the hell of Anorexia and later the isolation and secrecy of Bulimia. Although she still feels she has failed in practically all areas of her life Barbara has in fact achieved so much more than she could ever give herself credit for. She now supports other sufferers, raises money for the support network of which she is an active member, and cares for her six children single-handed. Here is her story...

My father had always been an alcoholic, and he had always been violent. Until I reached the age of seven, and my brother the age of four, he worked as a farm labourer. That benefited us because it meant he was out of the house for long periods at a time. For my mother, brother and myself that was a great relief, even if it was short-lived. But he then decided that he was not going to remain in employment any longer. He announced that he was going to live off the state instead. This was of course disastrous for the rest of us. His drinking became heavier and heavier and his temper more severe. Life at home became a living hell. There seemed no easy way to escape it. We felt trapped and desperate. My mum was too timid to stand up to my father. We were helpless.

Any money my father was given each week to care for his family was spent down at the pub. The rest of us saw very little of it. We often reached the stage when we became forced to beg from family and neighbours for food. We had nothing. When my father's money ran out he would start on my mother to find out where she had hidden the family allowance. He would always spend that as well. When drunk he would come home late at night, wake us up, and often throw us out into the street. The police would always find us a safe house to sleep in until my father had sobered up. It was a horrible existence.

When I was ten my Mum had to start work at a local factory because we desperately needed the small amount of income it would provide her with. She had recently had twins – a boy and a girl – so there were extra mouths to feed. As soon as Mum left the house each morning my father would go straight down to the pub, still hung-over from the previous day's drinking binge. I was left to look after myself, my brother and the twins. I feel now that I was given too much responsibility too early. I was forced to grow up when I was not ready. I was deprived of a childhood and I deeply resent that.

I remember late one Bonfire Night scouring the streets with the children in search of a bonfire for them to watch. It was dangerous being out so late at night alone. Anything could have happened to us but I did not want to disappoint the little ones. They deserved at least a little excitement in their lives.

We all witnessed so many traumatising events in the terrible years that followed. One example was the night I woke up to see my father, heavily drunk, holding a carving knife over my mother. He said he was going to kill her. I will never forget the feelings of panic and dread that rushed round my body. It was only the fact that a close relative appeared on the scene that prevented him from actually going ahead with his horrific threat.

On another occasion we locked him out of the house and he broke the front windows to get in. Once inside he started beating my mum. When I saw her glasses smash to the floor I went for him. I had to protect my mum. He was holding her round the throat and she was red in the face. I tried to drag him off her but I was just no match for his physical strength. He threw me across the room. I tried a second time to shield my mum from him but he hit me back with his hand. Then he held me by the neck, until I passed out. My brother, who had seen this happen, ran at that point to get the police. My five-year-old sister was screaming. Her twin brother stood in complete silence, shaking, lost in his own world.

That was the way life continued for many years until I was eventually able to break away. At the age of 17 I married and left home. I hoped this would mark the start of a new life for me away from the trauma that had been my home life. However, I was quick to discover that leaving home did not necessarily mean being able to leave behind the emotional trauma I had suffered there. That came with me – the feelings of neglect, the sense of worthlessness, the hopelessness, helplessness and despair. I had been left an 'emotional cripple.'

I soon found myself unable to cope with the pressures of day-to-day life. I became paranoid, convinced that everyone, including my husband, were saying nasty things about me. I hated myself and found it impossible to believe that anyone else could feel anything for me other than intense hatred. If my husband criticised me I took it extremely personally. It would upset me terribly. I would take it as a personal rejection. One day, when it all seemed too much, I made the decision to change myself. I thought about what I could do. My thoughts, feelings and attitude towards myself and towards life seemed too deeply entrenched to change, and so I decided to alter drastically my physical state instead. That would perhaps be more noticeable to my husband too. I decided that I would start dieting. I thought, rather naively, that becoming thin would be the answer to all my problems and that my husband would like me that way.

At this time I weighed nine stone. At a height of five foot four inches it could hardly be considered overweight. But I was desperate, and when you are desperate you are prepared to try anything. I gradually ate less and less until I was barely eating anything at all. The weight quickly fell off. The more I lost, the better I felt about myself. It gave me a real sense of achievement. I had gained strict control over one area of my life and that felt wonderful.

My husband worked shifts so the pair of us rarely ate together. As a result he remained, for a long time, completely unaware of what was going on. It was other family members that eventually started to make comments on my weight loss. It had become extreme by that stage. However, I saw their concern as interference and that was the last thing I wanted. They tried to force me to eat but I pushed them away. I wish now that instead of forcing me to eat they had forced me to see a counsellor. That was what I really needed, not food; food wasn't really the problem. I believe now that getting professional help at that stage would have prevented the years of suffering that followed.

During the start of this anorexic period I discovered that I was pregnant. I already had a son, born a year after our marriage, but I welcomed the chance to have another child. However my Anorexia was so strong that even the knowledge of this pregnancy could do nothing to halt my persistent starvation. Sadly, I lost the baby. I will have to live with that for the rest of my life. Shortly after that my husband left me. I took myself and my son to live with my mother. She had left my father, thankfully, and so it was safe to be with her. She welcomed the company as well. With my mother's care and support I was gradually able to increase my food intake.

As I said before, the real problem had never been food. I was using food to express my despair which had resulted from my father's drinking. I had started eating but of course the depression was still there. In fact without starvation it intensified, so I continued to abuse food. This time I ate but made myself sick afterwards. I discovered later that I had become bulimic. No one knew that I was making myself sick. They were all pleased that I was eating again and thought that I was fine, but inside I wasn't. As no one really knew what was going on I felt more alone than ever. Not surprisingly it was not long before I found myself another husband, someone to save me from my isolation.

The main thing I learnt from my first marriage was that although I could attack my own body through abusing food I would never again damage by unborn baby in that way. I had lost one, and if I ever got the opportunity to have another child, I would not ruin it this time. I did fall pregnant again, quite quickly, and remembered my determination not to starve this child. I was able to eat but I overcompensated. I did not know what 'normal' eating was and so I ate too much instead.

I ate and ate. I ended up at 14 stone and have been battling to lose it ever since. I produced a perfectly healthy baby which was a tremendous relief.

My second marriage was an absolute nightmare. The mental cruelty I endured from my husband beats description and is not something I would even want to consider thinking about. I remained with my husband for nine long years before managing to escape the marriage, only to fall headlong into another. That one lasted only four months.

I now have six children. Although I am on my own I survive on their love. They are all extremely precious to me. For a time eating disorders were a comfort to me but now the Bulimia I am left with has become the enemy. It makes my life hell. I have visited my doctor several times and begged for some help with it but each time I am sent away with nothing. My father is dead now. The drink finally killed him in the end. Sadly the pain and suffering he put me through did not go to the grave with him, but I will fight on. I fight this hell for the sake of my children. It breaks my heart to think of the distress I must have caused them. I have ruined their childhood. All their memories of me will be of an obese depressed mother. I dread to think of the damage I have done to them emotionally. I was selfish in having so many children but I just wanted people to love me and need me. I was selfish; I should have been able to offer them more. My children keep me going. I know they need me and so I will always be there for them.

My every thought is about food and its threat to me. I want to be happy and have a life. I hate food and I hate my body. I wish I could love it but I can't. The thing about Anorexia is that it is physically visible and so people can see what you are going through. With Bulimia that is not the case and so you suffer in silence. The isolation is unbearable at times. If someone passed me walking down the street they would never guess I had an eating disorder, but I wish they would; I would welcome that interference now.

Since writing this piece Barbara has found a doctor who is prepared to help her and through contact with other sufferers has found the support she needs. She has made considerable progress and is more in control of her eating problems now than she has ever been in the past.

CHAPTER 12

Shrieking, Crying and Insane Laughter

'Anorexia turned me into the daughter from hell.'

Cherry has experience of both Anorexia and Bulimia. She has endured a considerable amount but has survived, at times only because her thoughts were for other people such as her two children, and not for herself. She has suffered a great deal of loss and rejection but has come through it all. She feels, as many eating disorder sufferers do, guilty because she has survived when many more have not. Her sadness is for the loss of what those people would have contributed to the world. She feels she has survived but can contribute nothing. Nothing can be further from the truth. Cherry's story is frank and honest and the overall message is of survival, survival when the odds are stacked against you and people expect you to fail.

I am 44 years old, the mother of two children, and my name is Cherry. I have spent 28 years of my life consumed by an obsession with food so strong that I would rather commit suicide than allow anyone to control my eating. Even the thought terrifies me.

I never felt as if I fitted in anywhere as a child. I knew other children and carried out activities with them, but I never had a real friend apart from my Nan (Dad's Mum). She accepted me unconditionally. As for my parents, they were proud of my swimming trophies, my Guide's certificate, my academic prowess and my 'good deeds' to the less fortunate. I was a good and obedient child.

At 15 my parents made me move from Devon, where my Nan still lived, to a town in Kent that I perceived as snobby, and not the sort of place I wanted to live. There was no-one there to listen to me. I hated

Kent from the very first day I was there. I could no longer walk down the road and visit my Nan. I could not sit the nine 'O' Levels I had been studying for. I was no longer a school prefect or senior librarian. I could no longer attend the church, Guide company, swimming team or Brownie pack that I used to attend regularly. Kent had taken so much away from me; there was nothing familiar left. The form teacher at my new school took an immediate dislike to my broad Devonshire accent and said that 'one had to talk correctly at one's new school'. I was also very naive to the ways of the world and this brought a lot of ridicule. My Gran (Mum's Mum) later moved in with us and the house was permanently filled with arguments.

At 16 I started work as a laboratory assistant. I also started dating. My first love left me after just a few months. I was absolutely devastated. If I had been more confident about myself at the time I would have just put it down to experience. Instead I was left feeling fat, ugly and disgusting. I can now recognise that I was, in fact, fit and muscular, and the right weight for my height and build. My Gran started twisting the knife, causing me to get into trouble with my parents for things I had not done. She would also tell me how much my parents hated me. She said I had destroyed my mother's life. I grew to hate my parents as a result of this and we argued over everything. After a while I stopped eating and this seemed to make things a lot better. I was on a high and in control and, unusually for me, I did not care that I was nasty to them. I wanted them to suffer because I erroneously believed that they did not love me.

I carried on working and did not allow myself to feel weak. At home I pushed myself to exercise more. My parents soon noticed that something was wrong and they took me to see the doctor. My doctor was as easy to fool as my parents. They all believed I was eating sufficiently and therefore could not understand why I was losing weight. When I reached a weight of six stone my parents changed doctors to get another opinion on my situation. The new doctor made me see a psychiatrist. I still continued to lose weight. The psychiatrist would weigh me each time I went to see him but I don't think he ever knew my real weight because I always drank so much water before seeing him. One day, however, I passed out at home. My parents put me to bed and it was at that point that they saw how skinny I really was. My father contacted the Medical Officer for Health immediately to insist that something was done with me. I was carted off to a mental hospital very quickly. I screamed all the way there until they sedated me. I was full of panic and extreme anger.

When I arrived at the hospital I thought I had entered hell. There were people there whom I could only describe as walking vegetables. In fact there was no one there who looked as if they were capable of feeling, a state I soon got to know as 'cloud cuckoo land', although I never discovered why. I was terrified. I saw nurses coming round and making the patients take tablets and then have injections. They told me that all I had to do was eat but they gave me pills as well. I said that I didn't what them and that I wanted to go home but no one listened. At night it got worse, the wailing and shrieking and laughter really got to me. I kept thinking that I was not 'mental' so what on earth was I doing here? I was put in a side room on my own, they shut the door and I cried.

At first I was prescribed bedrest which the nurses made sure of by the use of medication. I soon got to know the names of the masses of chemicals they forced into me without my permission: sleeping pills, largactil, amitriptyline, insulin, iron, vitamins. Then came the ones that they would not tell me the names of nor would they tell me what they were for. I now believe that they were being tested on me, as after all I was mentally ill and so did not have any rights.

I was forced to eat and then I was violently sick. That was when the penny suddenly dropped. I realised that I could now eat anything, vomit it up afterwards and still lose weight. I started to save the food I was given and eat it at night so that I could vomit without being noticed (the night staff were far less vigilant). When I reached about four stone and I had become too exhausted to eat let alone vomit I was threatened with Electric Shock Treatment and a lobotomy if I did not eat. I was so scared that I really tried.

I am sure that my parents went through hell. I was not supposed to survive. The other two anorexic girls on the ward died but for some reason I started fighting. My Dad visited me every night even though I was not aware he was there most of the time. Mum hated the place and I don't remember her visiting much, but it might have been because she gave birth to a son while I was in hospital and I never knew. He was mentally and physically disabled and died before he was a year old. I never met him or even knew of his existence until a nurse mentioned it in passing. I had taken an overdose because I just could not stand the fact that I was putting on weight and had ended up being taken to casualty. When I became conscious some days later the nurse told me that my father had gone to visit my brother and would be along later. I had not even known that I had a brother! It was a horrible way to find out. Apparently the psychiatrist had said to my parents that I should not be told. At one stage my father, after work, was visiting my mother, my brother and me, and we were all in different hospitals. If he was not such a strong man he would surely have had a nervous breakdown.

I started putting on more weight and could not stop thinking about food. I craved it like an addict craves drugs. I also did not know why I felt ill or why I could not stop my eyes staring at the ceiling or even focus them. When I asked the nurse I was told that it was because I was ill; I have since discovered that it is a side effect of the largactil.

Some three years later, weighing six stone, I left the hospital, supposedly cured. I had to attend a day-centre every day. My behaviour gradually became even more bizarre, even to the extent of stealing food from the waste bin. The hospital obviously did not find out because they eventually released me. I had thought that Anorexia was difficult to live with but at least I was in control; with Bulimia I just could not stop eating and vomiting. I thought about food all the time and spent a lot of money on it. When I could not afford it I stole. I was out of control for the first time in my life and I honestly thought that I was insane. I even attempted suicide; I could stand it no longer.

At last however I met an older man; we married but I carried on bingeing and vomiting without him being any the wiser. At twenty-five I became pregnant and was lucky enough to deliver a healthy baby. I say lucky because I was still bulimic and my weight never increased throughout my pregnancy. After the birth I suffered Post Natal Depression and started to mutilate myself; I also attempted suicide. I was never told what I was suffering from – all I was told was, 'take these pills and you will be all right'. I wasn't all right. I discovered what had been wrong with me after reading an article about the illness.

Shortly after this my husband met someone else and left me; looking back I do not blame him as I hated sex and my body, in fact it was revulsion not hatred. My daughter and I were alone and I loved those years. I went out to work each day and when I came home I would play with her until she went to bed. Then I would binge and vomit. For some reason when I vomited it felt as if I was purging my body of everything evil that was inside. After vomiting I felt pure for a while, until the self-loathing took over.

Some six years later I married again and later, when I fell pregnant, I stopped vomiting for the sake of my unborn child. Somehow I could not face starting again. My weight soared to 19 stone and I couldn't face life, but I had to. My husband had found someone else and was gone. I was now alone again with two children who were completely dependent on me. The crazy thing was that the women he went off with was an alcoholic who was violent to others and to her children who, incidentally, were put into care. This made me feel even worse about myself as I had tried to be a good mother, and although I was fat I tried to look good and I was always clean and obedient, yet my husband had wanted this other woman more.

Under the guidance of a Community Psychiatric Nurse I lost weight until I reached ten stone which I am still at now; I say ten but in reality it is somewhere between nine and eleven stone, depending on when I am bingeing and when I am not eating at all.

Every night before I go to bed I pray that God will take pity on me and put me out of my misery, but he doesn't and somehow or other I can't commit suicide; the time for doing that was before I became responsible for the well-being of my two children.

I wish I knew why I became anorexic because I feel so guilty at the way in which my family have suffered, but I do not really believe that actually knowing would help in any way. The reason why I became anorexic is not applicable anymore because I am now an adult and I cannot continue to use food as a coping mechanism. I have to face up to my responsibilities to myself – I have neglected them for so long. I hate to admit it though but I think perhaps I wanted my family to suffer and feel guilty. I felt unloved and unwanted although I am now able to accept that my parents did, and still do, love me. When I was anorexic I was obnoxious, saying what I felt in a way designed to cause hurt to others, but my father still visited me at the hospital each night. I did not know how to stop being awful although I really did want to. Before

I became ill I had always been very well-behaved. Anorexia turned me into the daughter from hell.

At the time I had no close friends to talk to about how I felt and what was happening to me. Maybe I felt that I was not a good enough person to have friends. I thought that if I got ill I would be given sympathy. In my dreams there would always be a scene where I was dying and my family were crying and asking for forgiveness. I now accept that my parents did not know what was happening with my Gran, and that she was too mentally sick herself to care about what she was doing or the effect she was having on others.

My father lost promotion chances because he felt he could not leave the area. He wanted to be able to visit me. My sister, who is 11 years younger than me, also has an eating problem and we really do not know each other. I was too wrapped up in my own eating problems to be with her as she grew up. I also feel a certain amount of guilt that I may have contributed to her problems or even been the cause of them.

My Gran has asked me, in the last few years, if I will forgive her. What else can I say to a frail old lady except 'Yes' but I don't forgive her. I feel sorry for her and would help her all I could, but I cannot forgive her as with her help I have lost twenty-eight years of my life.

Apart from the eating problems and the knowledge of the damage I have done to myself, and that I'm still doing, physically, I worry continually about osteoporosis. Then there are the nightmares that I still suffer in times of stress, when I relive being in the hospital and I hear that awful shrieking and insane laughter. I think you need to have heard that noise to understand fully what I mean as words cannot describe it. This memory keeps me from being honest with any counsellor I see because I fear, deep down, being locked up again. My logical mind tells me that eating disorders are treated better now and that this would not happen again but I am scared to test the water, just in case. Not all anorexics survive their illness. I often feel guilty that the world has lost such people and that I have survived yet can offer the world nothing.

Sometimes I feel that I am two different people, the person I am when I do not eat, who is good, kind, considerate, in control of her life, happy and full of energy (I think it is called an adrenaline high) and the other person who has to lock herself away from the world and does not care about anything. She has to eat to let the carbohydrates sedate her feelings. The crazy thing, that is difficult to understand, is that I cannot let these two people merge into one; they have to remain separate from each other in the same way that my eating does, good and bad, black and white, separate. I cannot have bad thoughts when I am not eating, in the same way as I cannot eat and pollute myself on those days. Yes, I know I'm not cured and that my thoughts are irrational, and yes, I do wish they were different, but I am not brave enough to join them together for fear that no one will like the me that no one meets.

Anorexia and the Power of the Mind

'I kept begging God to take me but he obviously did not want me then.'

Derine's story shows very clearly the power of the human mind in the development of Anorexia and also in its recovery stages. It raises the point, often debated, that anorexics have to want to get better to gain anything from their treatment. As Derine explains, she had several hospital admissions which resulted in rapid weight gain. She would then return home and on each occasion lose all the weight she had gained, making the time spent in hospital useless, and putting her health in more danger. She did not want to get better.

The second point that Derine's story raises is the fact that anorexics do not need just to be fed. Anorexia is not solely a physical problem; if it was then once the sufferer had reached a healthy weight the problem would be solved. If that anorexic still has the same anorexic way of thinking then, as in Derine's case, the weight will simply not be allowed to stay on. Psychotherapy is therefore crucial to the sufferer's recovery. Understanding, of the illness and of what is going on for sufferers at that particular time in their lives, is needed. Only then will the anorexic be able to deal with problems and start thinking about life without the strict control of food that seems so important for survival. If they see an end to their problems and have hope for the future the will-power to get better will gradually develop. As is obvious, anorexics have the determination to achieve anything they want – if they put their mind to it.

I was anorexic for almost 28 years and during that time I can't remember ever being really happy. Several times the illness nearly killed me. Before my last hospitalisation I really hoped I would die – life had become so unbearable.

I first became anorexic about ten months after my marriage. I loved my husband but circumstances surrounding us were not ideal. He lived with his mother which was not a good start, and we both worked all hours in our respective businesses and therefore spent little time together, time that was really necessary to cement our relationship. I became very depressed over the situation and started over-eating. Hitherto I'd possessed a normal appetite and my weight had been nine stone two pounds all my teenage years until I was about 22 years old. My husband owned a general store – with his mother – and after I had finished for the day at the hairdressing business I ran I would go over to his shop, arm myself with bars of chocolate and other snacks, go back to my shop and scoff the lot. About two hours later I would prepare, cook (picking at things while I went along) and eat an evening meal. I was secretly stuffing myself. This continued all day every day for several months. I hated it. I hated myself and I hated the inevitable weight gain that went with the bingeing. I put on a stone in a few months in spite of discovering laxatives and using them in an attempt to shift the weight.

This all took place in the 1960s and at that time little was known by the general public about calories and calorific values. However it was not long before a diet was drawn up which involved counting the number of calories one ate for the day, according to height and weight etc. I thought it sounded a great idea and decided at once to attempt it. Other diets had failed so I felt that it deserved a chance. By this time I had become desperate to end the bingeing which had become quite uncontrollable at times. I never vomited but it was still a nightmare. So I started on this calorie-counted diet, along with many other women, I expect. I really got on well with it because it allowed me to decide what to do with the 1240 calories I was allowed to have. I would give myself a treat at the end of the day by keeping 100 calories for anything I fancied – what luxury!

I must point out at this stage that all my overeating, dieting and misery was kept a closely guarded secret. Never at any time did I even hint at what I was doing. I would have been very upset if anyone else had known anything about what was going on. My husband liked me at ten stone, I had been eight and a half stone when we married. When he noticed my weight loss, at around eight stone, he was not keen. The opposite in fact. As for me, I loved it! The dieting gave me a purpose in life, something to strive for which I found really exciting and stimulating. It had become a real challenge – to see how much weight I could lose. I also enjoyed counting calories. When we went a restaurant I would immediately select my limit from the menu and felt good about sticking to it while enjoying the meal. I was taking laxatives at the time and had reached the unfortunate stage when accidents were likely, and so I needed to be near a toilet at all times. I also suffered the most dreadful stomach cramps but gradually began to accept them as part of my existence.

Throughout all this I always felt as though the situation was only temporary and would all come to an end in the unseen, vague future. I was convinced I was in control of the situation. How wrong I was!

During the following few months I continued to diet. I kept telling myself that if I stopped and put weight on it would not matter too much because I had already lost more weight than I had intended to lose. I wanted to go down to eight stone as I felt so much more lively when I weighed less. I convinced myself that the less I weighed and the less I ate, the better I would feel both physically and mentally. This belief fuelled my determination to lose weight. The weight loss continued. I soon reached the stage where I had gone beyond dieting and was starving. I began to feel really ill. I suffered dreadfully as a result of the regular laxative abuse. I had constant diarrhoea, but I just could not make myself change my habits; they had become a way of life.

Naturally my husband was very worried. He kept taking me to the doctor. Anorexia Nervosa was diagnosed but nothing was done about it. My husband then insisted that I see a psychiatrist. An appointment was made for me. Within a few days I was admitted into a psychiatric hospital for the first of a long series of hospital admissions in a variety of hospitals.

The first visit was for eight weeks during which time I was put on bedrest 24 hours a day for six weeks in total. I was given increased dosages of largactil to stimulate my appetite and induce constant sleep. I remember being given three huge meals a day, plus three snacks, and being scarcely able to feed myself – I was just too dozy. During the next few years I went in and out of hospitals for varying lengths of time. On each occasion I was given huge meals plus three hefty snacks and my weight increased sufficiently to allow me to be discharged. Once back at home I would just return to my dieting and laxative abuse because I hated my extra weight. I would feel bloated and full to bursting point and I could not stand it; it was an awful feeling.

In one hospital I was given a great deal of psychiatric treatment. This helped me to understand what was going on with me. Previously it had all been very confusing and difficult to rationalise in my mind. I began to realise that this self-punishment was a way of compensating for the lack of joy in my life. I had not been happy as a child and my marriage had not brought me the love and support I so desperately needed in order to flourish. Resorting to starvation was my way at getting back at myself and the world for the fact that I felt I had had a raw deal. After 12 years of marriage my husband gave up on me and went to live with someone else. Our marriage was over.

I was very upset, to say the least. I felt so alone. Although I still had a good hairdressing business I had very little else in my life. I fell into a deep depression that lasted for nearly a year. Then I came to the realisation that I needed to get out and meet people. I just could not continue living the half-life I had been living; things had to change. I pursued my interest in music and singing and gradually started going out socially. One boyfriend followed another. Not one of them guessed that I had an eating disorder. My weight wavered between six and seven stone for several years until I met someone that I began to care for a great deal. But he let me down badly. He returned to his estranged wife after two-timing me with someone else! I couldn't believe it. I went downhill a lot after that.

I had practically stopped eating altogether and my weight plummeted to four stone two pounds. I was admitted into hospital yet again. This time I was treated very severely because my life was in extreme danger. I was put on complete bedrest; all my possessions were taken away on a punishment/reward system where if you did something 'good', such as eat a meal, you were rewarded by being given back one of your possessions. If you did something 'bad' it was taken away again. I put on four stone in eight weeks under that regime. I then returned home to lose it all again.

Over the years my Anorexia persisted, in spite of all the hospital admissions I'd had after numerous relapses. I *did* want to get better. By the beginning of 1996 I was really ill again, so much so that I could not walk very easily and I could only do the most basic of things. I was really only capable of washing and dressing myself. I could not manage to cook when I wanted to and so I ended up living on toast and drinks.

Friends and family were very kind at the time and I am most grateful to them. They helped me in every way they could. Finally my mother and brother pushed so hard for me to go into hospital that I was forced to go in again. Just prior to this I had made several attempts to end my life, to get away from the anorexic hell I was living in. I just could not live with myself or the illness any longer. I kept begging God to take me but he obviously did not want me then. Shortly after being admitted into hospital I began what proved to be my cure.

It was not at all easy-going through the enforced feeding and close observation, but after nine weeks in two consecutive hospitals I came home a stone and a half heavier. From the four-and-a-half stone wreck I had been when I went in, I came out very near my target weight of seven stone. For the first time I was really thrilled at my weight gain. I felt better than I had felt in a long time and I knew I was on the road to recovery. I had been anorexic for so long that I had reached the stage where I was desperate to get better; the weight gain was half the battle, and there was only another 50 per cent to go.

During my time in hospital I had also been able to do a lot of thinking, to reflect on the past few years and to think about what I wanted from my life. I wanted to be well and when I was discharged I was determined to get well and stay well.

I still have my problems but they are mild in comparison. I am fit, healthy and happy. I love my life now and I enjoy every day. Even the unpleasant things that life throws at me I tackle with enthusiasm. I see my difficulties as a challenge and I overcome them.

Anorexia is all in the mind. To get well you have to want to be well. Once you are well you have to be determined to stay that way. The world has not changed; you will still be faced with problems and difficulties every day. The factors that triggered your eating problems may still be there but you have to deal with them effectively. Starving yourself to the point of near-death is certainly not the way to do it. I am so relieved that I will never have to go through that hell again. Anorexia is out of my head forever.

CHAPTER 14

The 'Problem Child'

'By reducing my body size I hoped I would no longer be seen as a sexual object that could be used and abused.'

The main theme of Helen's very powerful story is sexual abuse. It is an issue often linked to Anorexia Nervosa and Helen's experiences provide an example of an anorexic who has lost weight in order to get rid of her feminine characteristics and therefore lose all aspects of her sexuality. Any form of child abuse, and the resulting trauma the victim suffers, is a complex area of psychiatry and one that can be very difficult to treat. Victims find it difficult to admit and even more difficult to explain in detail the horrors they have been through. Helen too faced this problem. For anyone who reads Helen's story it is clear just how much she has suffered as a result of the attacks of her father, and the suffering has not started and ended with Anorexia. There is so much more to the suffering she has been through.

I think my problems actually started the day I was born. My father wanted a boy and so he was very disappointed when I arrived. My father hates women and I can fully understand why. When he was three years old his mother was very ill. He and the rest of his twelve brothers and sisters were sent off to live with other members of his family. My father went to an uncle and aunt. When his mother had regained her health, naturally she wanted her children back. However the uncle and aunt did not want this and so refused to hand my father back. They were a wealthy couple and believed they could give him a better upbringing. So my father remained with them and his mother sent a set amount of money to them each week.

Every time his mother tried to visit, my father was locked away in the attic of the house until she had gone. The couple refused to let him see her, together with the rest of his large family. He was given the best money could buy and went to the best schools. But he was deprived of one essential person – his mother. As a result of this he has grown into an angry person who hates women, his mother for abandoning him, and his aunt for trying to replace her when he should have been with his real family. That anger has been taken out, to a large extent, on me. Although I know he has had a tough childhood, I still hate him for what he has done to me. He has completely ruined my life.

It is very obvious to me that my father's actions have contributed greatly to my Anorexia. It is very difficult to put down on paper, but basically my father sexually abused me. Just like him I now wish I had never been born a girl. I will wish that for the rest of my life. If I had not been born a girl I would never have suffered the horrific abuse that began at the age of just three. At least that is my first memory of it. I am now 27. He beat me too, but that was not so bad as physical bruises heal in time while mental ones don't.

I developed Anorexia at the age of 13 although I feel I have had eating problems all my life. When you first fall ill you don't really know what is happening to you or why it is happening. Looking back on it now I am certain that, to an extent, I was trying to get rid of my feminine characteristics. By reducing my body size I hoped I would no longer be seen as a sexual object that could be used and abused. Losing weight made me look more asexual, more boyish.

My weight dropped so much that I was admitted to hospital. They diagnosed me as having Anorexia Nervosa. I started putting on weight in hospital and soon reached the weight they wanted me to be. I relapsed, however, after being discharged and I do not think the after-care they provided was adequate. Although I did see a psychiatrist on a regular basis I found it so difficult to talk. I found it easier to write things down but I realise now that there were things I needed to say, about the abuse in particular, just to hear myself say them. I wish now that I had been pushed more to talk; there was so much I needed to say. I have done a lot of soul-searching recently. I have been trying to work out why I became ill and why I am still suffering today.

I don't think the hospital had the resources to provide the outpatient therapy that I so desperately needed. As far as they were concerned I had reached their required weight and that was that, end of story, except sadly it wasn't. My parents had the finances to pay for such help but they were not prepared to. They dismissed my eating disorder as just a little problem. They refused to acknowledge my depression at all. Instead they spent their money on textbooks for my schooling but that made things worse. The pupils at school teased me for this and I was termed a 'snob.' My parents' wealth really made me stick out and I was an easy target for the bullies. It was a very rough school so there were plenty of them. I was often threatened with knives if I did not hand over money. They ripped my clothes and stole books. Life at school became nearly as bad as life at home.

Becoming anorexic and focusing on food and weight was a form of escapism from the trauma of my life. It seemed to be the solution to a lot of my problems and gave me a sense of control. My problems seemed out of my control but what I ate and what I weighed was within my control. It also gave me a sense of achievement and enjoyment. I hated life at school and I hated life at home. But what I did enjoy was losing weight.

Being in hospital was difficult but it was a relief to be away from my father. He was the main cause of my problems and I had been so desperate to get away from him. No one knew that he was abusing me because I had not told anyone – I just couldn't bring myself to say it. I also hated all the arguing that took place at home between my parents. They were always threatening each other with divorce but never went ahead with it. When my father suddenly lost his job the arguing and shouting continued all day because he was home. Once my mother threw a knife at him. He had to go to hospital to have a wound in his head stitched. It was dreadful. My mother left home that day but returned after just a few days away. The arguments continued just like before.

There have been times when my father has left me alone and has in fact said reasonably nice things to me and bought me presents. But it never lasts; in fact I am convinced he bought me things to blackmail me emotionally into getting what he wanted from me. I hated it so much that one day I took an overdose but later at school I collapsed and was rushed to hospital. I had not done any major harm and was discharged the following day. My parents did not understand why I had taken the overdose and just told me what a terrible person I was and how much I had let them down. I had seen a psychiatrist during my time in the hospital but I was completely unable to answer his questions. I was just too scared to tell him about my father. I already felt too much of a failure as far as my family were concerned so I said nothing. It was then assumed that I was attention-seeking. My parents took me home and lectured me again. Then my father beat me. I felt completely worthless, unwanted, unloved. My life felt completely beyond my control. I stopped eating. Nobody even noticed.

I had soon established a routine to my day. My parents were getting on a little better which helped. They were busy with their retail business and so did not have much time to focus on anything or anyone other than themselves. Each day I would go to school, come home and prepare the evening meal, then do my homework before serving dinner. When everyone had finished eating I would wash up and then do a little more housework. Nobody ever noticed that I never sat down and ate something myself.

I lost a stone, two stone…and so it continued. My clothes started hanging off me as they had become far too big. Still nobody noticed until the day when once again I collapsed at school. It was hard to convince people that I had not taken another overdose. They wanted to send for an ambulance but I insisted that I was all right. I continued living each day after that feeling like a complete zombie. I had so little energy that I could barely do anything. I coped for another six weeks before collapsing again. One of my teachers, I'll call him Mr Jones, was a medical aid. He picked me up off the floor and told me later that he had known immediately what was wrong with me. I was so light.

I sat and cried in his office while he tried to convince me that I needed medical help. I told him about the bullying I was having to endure at school but nothing of the trauma of my home life. Mr Jones made a deal with me. I agreed to start eating again and see a psychiatrist and he agreed not to tell my parents. But I was crafty even at that stage. I had agreed to *see* a psychiatrist but not to actually talk to him!

I did start eating again and I sat with Mr Jones for lunch each day so that he could witness me eating. It never occurred to me to make myself sick and get rid of it. It didn't seem to matter at that stage. I had found a friend, someone that wanted to know me, and I felt a little happier. My sessions with the psychiatrist soon ended though. He said that there was no point in me seeing him if I was not prepared to say anything. Mr Jones was great about it despite our original deal. I started talking to him instead and slowly I began to trust him. I told him about my parents' constant arguing, but not about the abuse.

Mr Jones sorted out the bullies. I became known as a teacher's pet as well as a snob but I didn't care. Life continued and things were a little easier, thank goodness, but then at the age of 15 my father made me pregnant. I got myself into such a state about the whole thing that I slit my wrists. I had to see another psychiatrist. Shortly afterwards I lost the baby.

Life went rapidly downhill after that. I hated school and I hated everything; I'd had enough of living the life everyone else wanted me to live. I felt like a slave at home, doing the housework, the cooking and so on…and having to put up with my father continually raping me.

I started playing truant from school. I was past the point of caring. I had no idea where my life was heading, or even what I was doing half the time. The school contacted my parents about my absences which resulted in their lecturing me again and my father beating me. I returned to school but I had no interest in my studies whatsoever. Inevitably my grades fell drastically but I did not care. My moods fluctuated greatly. I no longer wanted to live. I felt there was no life for me. I took another overdose but once again survived. The usual routine of having to see psychiatrists continued but this time it was different. The psychiatrist I met said that it didn't matter to him whether I spoke or not and encouraged me to write my feelings down on paper.

I wrote down a lot of things and it really helped but I was still unable to mention the abuse. In fact the abuse had got worse. It was no longer just my father that had taken an interest in my body; my brother had also become interested. He too raped me several times. I was unable to fight him off – he was so much stronger than me. My attempts to get rid of my feminine characteristics had clearly failed.

I hated my father, I hated my brother, but more than anything I hated myself. Not surprisingly I failed all my 'O' Levels. My parents were disgusted. Once again I had let the family down. My father said I was a waste of space and that he could not understand why. He said that neither my brother nor my sister had caused so much trouble. From that point onwards he always referred to me as the 'problem child'.

I moved to a new college to retake my exams but it was extremely difficult. It was a strict college run by priests. I found it so hard to make friends. The other pupils seemed very different from the ones I was used to and I found myself permanently on my guard. There wasn't really any need to be; I just found it impossible to relax. To make matters worse I could not see my psychiatrist. The college was in a different area and therefore too far away. I felt abandoned, lonely and very depressed.

It was a long train journey to the college and I found myself using food in a different way; this time I started comfort eating. I ate large amounts of sugary, fattening food with little care about my figure. It wasn't until I visited my grandmother that I realised I had put a lot of weight on. With shock and surprise in her voice she told me just how *fat* I was. I weighed myself and I was ten stone. I was horrified and felt absolutely disgusting. I immediately went on a fat- and sugar-free diet. I also exercised in my free time. Even when I was supposed to be studying I exercised. The weight came off fairly easily and I got thinner. But still I dieted and exercised. Eventually it began taking over my life.

One of the girls that I had come to regard as a friend suddenly died. She had been abroad and had caught something. It was completely unexpected. I was in a complete state of shock; I just could not come to terms with her death. I couldn't handle my grief. I felt that she should not have been the one that died — it should have been me. I deserved to die but she certainly didn't. I blamed myself for her death. I talked to one of the priests but he just was not able to understand. I was left feeling completely devastated. I have never been able to come to terms with her death.

I decided I wanted to die. I wrote a long suicide letter and left it where it would be found after my death. I then went to the church to pray for forgiveness for what I was about to do. But the principal found me before I had time to take anything. The college counsellor was called. I talked to her. My words were full of intense pain and anger. For the first time I spoke about the abuse. I was in a terrible state afterwards. She couldn't calm me down; I wanted to be alone so I left and went home. Meanwhile the counsellor called my parents and told them everything I had told her in confidence. I couldn't believe it. My mother beat me when I got home. Later when I was alone my father came in and said that no matter what I said about him and no matter to whom I said it he would always deny it. Then he beat me.

I passed my 'O' levels and went on to study for my 'A' Levels. I got in with the crowd at school and was introduced to drink, drugs and alcohol. When my parents found out they made me work with them in one of their shops. I had to spend so much time with them and I was miserable. Then my world shattered around me when I discovered that once again I was pregnant.

The bigger and bigger I got the more I wanted to keep the baby but I was afraid to tell my parents I was pregnant. I had tried to hide my bump under baggy clothes. I did not know how they would react to the news. I was four and a half months pregnant when my father came home completely drunk. He came into the house shouting abuse. He began beating my mother. I instinctively went to help her but then he turned on me. I lost my balance and fell down the stairs. I felt a lot of pain and began to bleed. Later that night I went into labour.

I told my mother what was wrong and she helped to deliver the baby. The baby was a little girl. She was beautiful and perfect in every way except that she did not move. My little baby was dead. My mother took her away from me and I never saw her again. I was so gutted and angry that such a precious life could be destroyed by one punch too many. The baby's life could never be celebrated. She was never even recognised as being born. She has no birth certificate, no funeral, no proper burial, no grave. Today I am not even allowed to speak of her.

Life in the house continued as normal. Eventually I was well enough to get a job and so I became a radiographer. But at that time I had not realised how stressful it would be. I was working with very sick people all the time and that is not easy for anyone to cope with. There was also pressure from hospital management to improve performance percentages. I couldn't cope with the pressure and slowly began to crack under the pressure. I stopped eating.

Every so often I would have the urge to eat but when I did I would make myself sick afterwards. The more weight I lost the more depressed

I became until I reached the point where I thought dying was the only way out. I took an overdose and ended up back in hospital. The nurses were supportive; they seemed to understand the pressure I had been under and how difficult it was.

My contract at the hospital was not renewed, probably due to my depression, so I moved to work at a different hospital. But I ended up with the same problems as of course I was doing the same line of work and clearly it was not suited to me. The cycle of starvation and overdoses continued. I met another psychiatrist. This time I was able to talk. I liked him. He put me at ease. I even told him about the abuse in as much detail as I was able. It was difficult but with him there I felt I was getting somewhere. I slowly began to eat.

Things were looking better than they had looked for a long time but then my psychiatrist suddenly announced that he was leaving. He would not be able to see me anymore. I was gutted. I lost weight and ended up in hospital. I was very depressed while I was there but they discharged me anyway and I was relieved to go. Then I began to binge. I was lonely and depressed and once again started to eat for comfort. I was not able to get rid of it all by making myself sick. It was then that I heard about laxatives and so I started to abuse them in the hope that it would reduce my weight.

After a while I was diagnosed as being bulimic. Various medical appointments inevitably followed and more psychiatrists. I went back to a psychiatrist I had seen previously. He seemed concerned for me and it helped to see him. I wasn't really able to talk about my problems but I was able to write him long letters and he agreed to that.

Life has continued much like that ever since. I write to my psychiatrist every day and that is a lifeline I really need. I still get extremely depressed. I see no light at the end of the tunnel. I despise myself and the way I have let food ruin my life. I'd like things to change but if the recent past is anything to go by they won't. But where there's life there's hope. Or so they say.

CHAPTER 15

Food, Tablets, Blades and Drink

'The realisation that I could help others helped me to help myself.'

Rachel's account raises many issues, in particular the dangers of over-feeding Anorexics during a period of hospitalisation. Naturally sufferers need to gain weight but this weight needs to be gained in a carefully controlled way that the anorexic can cope with. This did not happen in Rachel's case and she ended up in a cycle of bingeing so severe that she tried to take her own life. There is a fine line between Anorexia and Bulimia. Uncontrolled over-feeding in hospital can lead to bingeing which can lead to Bulimia.

When I was 16 years old my parents decided to move from our home in Derbyshire to St. Andrews in Scotland. I had just left school at the time and was in my first serious relationship which had lasted for almost a year. I did not want to move but due to a lot of emotional pressure I did. Shortly after arriving in Scotland I started college in Dundee. I was severely depressed and very lonely. I would cry all night in my room and count the days until I visited my boyfriend again. Due to my unhappiness, my parents and I argued a lot. This only made matters worse, I felt distant from them and therefore even lonelier.

After four months my boyfriend decided that he had had enough of our long-distance relationship and so we split up. I was devastated. From that moment on I just could not bear to eat. I hated the thought of having something in my mouth. For a whole week I ate nothing, and as I was overweight at the time this resulted in me losing a stone in weight. I thought this was great and so I starved myself for another week. I lost nothing. Depressed but determined not to give up, I increased my intake a little so that my metabolism would not slow down too much. This increase worked and I began to lose weight again. That helped me to feel better.

About a month later my parents finally agreed to let me move back to Derby. I began living with my aunt and went to the local college which all my friends attended. My life changed completely. I felt a lot happier. I enjoyed nights out and enjoyed meeting guys. I got two part-time jobs which kept me busy after college and I soon had my ex-boyfriend wanting me back! He begged me but I was just not interested any more. My weight loss continued during this time. I was very aware of what I ate but at least once in a while I would let my hair down and have a drink and a 'naughty' treat. At this stage my dieting was part of my life, but not my whole life.

It was during the summer, while on a family holiday, that my dieting really took over my life and I became totally obsessed. I refused to eat almost everything and would only drink diet drinks that contained less than one calorie per can. Any more than that and I just would not drink it. I spent hours gazing at cake shop windows, chocolate bars and cookery books. I would cook delicious meals for my family but would not eat any of it myself. I even applied to catering college to do a chef's course.

A year after my Anorexia began I weighed just five and a half stone. I had originally been 15 stone so I had lost approximately two thirds of my body weight. I was very ill indeed. My legs were swollen and looked as if they would burst open at any moment. I could hardly walk. I finally realised I needed help when one day I sat down on the toilet seat and just could not get up again. I cried for hours after that and begged my family to help me.

The next day my sister and I travelled to my parents' house in Scotland where their GP admitted me into a general hospital. I stayed in this hospital for two weeks before being transferred to a local psychiatric hospital. Once in hospital I lost total control of my eating habits. I ate all day every day. I just could not wait to eat all of the things I had been dying to eat for so long. People were so pleased to see me eating again that they encouraged the bingeing by bringing whatever treats I asked them for. The weight inevitably piled on at an amazing rate and I began to panic. However I just could not control my intake no matter how hard I tried. It was then that I decided to take laxatives. It was a desperate attempt to slow down the weight gain. Looking back I suppose it did help in a way but I was in constant agony and completely overcome with guilt.

My depression soon returned with a vengeance and I really wanted my life to be over, I just could not bear it any longer. I had decided that if I was going to be fat forever then I would much rather be dead. I took an overdose of paracetamol but was later discovered, wandering around the hospital grounds in a hysterical state. I was taken to hospital and had to have my stomach pumped. I was then put on a drip for two days. I felt like hell. My Mum hated me so much that she just could not bring herself to look at me for a few days. I still don't think she has ever forgiven me, eight years on, for what I put her through that night.

After this episode my belongings were searched and my laxatives discovered. The nursing staff then came to the conclusion that if I lost a bit of weight I would feel happier. They put me on a restricted diet. I hated it. I seemed unable to make them understand why it would not work. My bingeing had to continue in secret. I would sneak to the shops, stealing food whenever I could, and I got the other patients to get food for me as well. It was horrible. However, during this time I became very close to a male patient and we eventually got engaged. His attention lifted my mood considerably.

After seven and a half months in the hospital I was discharged. I went from there to a supported accommodation flat near my parent's home. For the first few months there I drank quite a lot and often needed to be carried home. This stopped however when I discovered that I was pregnant. Although worried, naturally, about my parents' reaction, I was happy about the pregnancy. My fiancé and I then decided to get married. At that point I felt very happy and thought that my problems were behind me. I was very wrong.

While pregnant I worried so much about the regular weigh-ins that I began to become over-concerned about my diet. I ended up losing a stone and a half during the pregnancy, but thankfully delivered a healthy baby girl. I was delighted to have a child but the weight loss still continued. By the time my daughter was nine months old I was in hospital again. I was very depressed, unable to eat with others, exercise-mad, and had taken to cutting myself with razor blades.

This hospital stay lasted a month, then I asked to leave. The boredom was making me worse, never mind the heartache of being without my baby. Around this time a new self-help group for people with eating disorders had been set up in my town. I joined and found it very helpful. The people there actually understood how I felt. I belonged somewhere at last. I also joined the Eating Disorders Association and found strength in others' experiences.

Not long after this my husband and I decided to move to his home town of Rochdale. We felt we needed to get away from my parents. They were very controlling and I felt trapped being so near them. This decision caused a major argument with my parents and we ended up not speaking for about three months. The house we moved into was an absolute dump and the landlord was not a very desirable character. We had made a massive mistake and we knew it. I became depressed and suicidal, and my husband, who was schizophrenic, had several acute attacks resulting in hospital admissions.

I returned to using food to control my emotions and developed compulsive eating patterns. Once more I ate all day every day and gained a considerable amount of weight. Everyone around me could see that I was letting myself go. I also returned to using razor blades and made some serious marks on myself as a result of deep cuts not being stitched. After one particular bout of self-harm my husband dragged me off to see the doctor who referred me to the local mental health team. Here is where I met Suzanne and Mandy. I did not realise then but my recovery had begun!

Mandy was my mental health worker and was based at the local resource centre. She spent hours talking to me, and was the first person to take everything I said seriously. She supported me in hours of crisis and encouraged me to do alternative things, other than abusing food and my body, when I felt depressed. With Mandy's guidance I started to write diaries and poems which helped me to get in touch with my feelings. She also helped me to set up my own self-help group – organising a room and funding from the resource centre where she worked. There were many occasions when she went out of her way to help me and the group. This group eventually got going in February 1994 and was extremely beneficial to me. I gained a lot of confidence and my self-esteem grew. The realisation that I could help others helped me to help myself.

Suzanne was my social worker. She helped me to sort out my housing, money, and many other basic things. She too listened and understood me, and to them both I will be forever grateful.

My recovery was finally complete when I returned to college to do an access to higher education course. This led to me meeting many other people and to being accepted onto a teacher training course at university – something I had always longed to do. Unfortunately (or fortunately) I could not take up my university place as I had become pregnant with my second child. Around the same time I also separated from my husband.

I now live back in Derby. I am a 23-year-old single mother of two beautiful daughters, and mostly I enjoy my life. My worries about my body and about food are still there, but they no longer dominate my life or cause me undue stress. In fact I now attend a naturalist park with my friends which I think is great – very liberating!!

I continue to try to help other sufferers by being a postal support for the Eating Disorders Association. This means I write with advice and support to other people who are suffering the hell of an eating disorder. I currently write to about five sufferers and I find their courage inspiring.

As for the problems that caused my Anorexia – my parents are still very much there, but my ability to cope with them grows stronger by the day. I have stopped trying to be something I am not – the person they had wanted me to be. I have accepted the person I am and have grown to like myself, most of the time. Now, at last, I am proud to be me!

CHAPTER 16

A Case of Denial or a
Self-Fulfilling Prophecy?

'There was no real reason why I wanted to lose weight. I think I had become addicted to it, addicted to the high I got from starvation and from seeing the scales go down and down.'

Elaine strongly rejects her diagnosis of Anorexia Nervosa. Her argument is that by being labelled an anorexic she felt she had to behave as such. She puts forward a strong argument but the fact remains that she did become severely anorexic. One would question how being misdiagnosed could possibly have made her so ill. If Elaine had not become anorexic it is possible that she would have expressed her problems using some other means. So, is Elaine completely denying the fact that her problems led to Anorexia, or was it really a case of a self-fulfilling prophecy? I leave it to the reader to decide.

When I was 15 years old I was labelled as anorexic. The fact is that I wasn't anorexic at all. I wasn't eating much – that much was true – but I did not have full-blown Anorexia. I believe that different types of personalities deal with food in different ways under intense pressure. There are certain people that turn to food for comfort when things get tough. There are others that lose their appetite. I am in that category. I always have been, even when I was very young and unaware of what I was really doing. When I'm stressed or unhappy I just lose the desire to eat. There is no anorexic thinking behind it. My intention is not to lose weight, I just don't feel like eating. When I am feeling better I get my appetite back and life carries on as normal.

When I was 15 I was busy studying for my GCSEs and I was very worried about the forthcoming examinations, as were most of my friends. I reached the point when I felt sick with nerves. The result was that I could not face food. I would eat the odd thing here and there, usually chocolate or a cake as I had a very sweet tooth. I could not face a big meal but on a diet of chocolate and cakes I managed to keep myself reasonably healthy. Most teenagers don't eat that healthily anyway, so my way of eating was not that unusual. However, my headteacher seemed to think it was. I only discovered this one day on arriving home and finding that he had called my mother saying he was very concerned about me because I never ate a meal at lunchtime. He had also said that he was concerned because I looked pale and thin.

The fact was that at that age I was naturally slim and I always had been. I had even been asked in the past by friends whether I was anorexic, that was how slim I was. But I had always eaten well and I loved my food. I had never weighed myself in my life; my weight just did not concern me. I had no idea of calories, had never dieted or even considered it, I certainly had none of the characteristics of an anorexic. In fact there was a girl in my year at school that I had heard was anorexic. I just could not understand the illness at all. I remember telling people, including my mother, just how stupid she was. I just could not understand how anyone could go without food, especially chocolate! To me it sounded like absolute torture, and certainly not something that I would want to try.

I still felt like that the day I arrived home to hear about the headmaster's phone call. I told my mother there was nothing to worry about but naturally she was concerned. Unfortunately that evening I could not face any dinner. I had eaten some chocolate on the way home. My first exam was so near that all I wanted to do was go to my bedroom and revise. I hadn't worked particularly hard at school as I did most of my work at night.

Life carried on much the same except for the fact that there were more confrontations at home about food. It angered me that a fuss was being made. I knew there was nothing wrong with me and that my eating would get back to normal once the pressure of my exams were over. I tried to make that clear but my parents did not seem to be able to understand.

Not surprisingly the situation at home got worse around the time of my exams because I was so tense and my parents were so anxious for me. They seemed to share my exam nerves but they were also concerned about my health. The exams passed more quickly than I had expected and it was an enormous relief when they were finally over. The world suddenly looked a much nicer place to live in and I felt so much happier. It was as if a massive weight had been taken off my shoulders. I felt quite high with it all but I was soon brought back down to earth the day after my exams had finished.

I had spent the morning out with friends shopping. We had all had a great time doing nothing much, just relaxing. We all got a burger and chips for lunch and I suddenly realised just how hungry I was so I ordered an extra serving. I felt as if I was starving. Just as anticipated my appetite had come back, in full force it seemed! I arrived home feeling happier and with much more energy. I was looking forward to the long holiday that lay ahead before school started again. I was looking forward to going back to study for my 'A' levels. I would be in the sixth form and I knew I would feel very grown up being able to wear my own clothes and not a school uniform.

I joined my mother in the kitchen for a coffee and noticed immediately that she did not look at all happy. She poured the drinks and I insisted on having mine black; I did not want any milk. I had got used to drinking black coffee in the evenings, to help me keep awake and alert, in order to revise. After several months on black coffee I had decided I preferred it to white. However my mother was convinced that I didn't want milk because it had more calories in it. Apparently she had bought a calorie book so that she could measure my daily intake. I discovered that later. The calories were not a problem to me. I was not even aware of them. It frustrated me terribly that my mother was convinced that I had a problem when I didn't. Looking back now it makes me angry because it was then that I started becoming more aware of the calorific value of food – all because my mother kept mentioning it. She was making me more conscious of what I was eating. I was developing an unhealthy attitude towards food.

It was a week later when I found the calorie book. She had hidden it in one of the kitchen cupboards. It was at the same time that I found a book on Anorexia Nervosa and some leaflets about the illness that she had got through the post. I had been about to eat a chocolate bar but instead I sat down and looked through the calorie book. I had never seen one before and it made interesting reading. I was horrified at the high level of calories in chocolate. I had not realised it was so fattening. I suddenly felt guilty for wanting to eat it. Then seeing that fruit had far fewer calories I put the chocolate bar away and chose an apple instead.

That evening I had decided that I would join the family for the evening meal. I thought that they would all be pleased. I had not sat at the table for a while. I had been too busy revising. However when I went into the dining room no place had been set for me. I felt left out and very upset. Moments later my mother said that she wanted me to take myself out for a couple of hours that evening. A family friend, who was also a doctor, was coming round to discuss my Anorexia with them. I was horrified. I did not have Anorexia. They were making their own diagnosis when there was absolutely nothing wrong with me. I was hungry and I wanted to eat. For the first time I hated them. I hated them for not listening to me and for labelling me with some psychiatric complaint that I certainly did not have. I saw the doctor arrive later that evening and left the house before he could see me. I would have felt embarrassed if he had caught sight of me because if he had been told I had an eating problem he was bound to expect me to be thin, but I wasn't; I was normal.

I got on my bike and cycled down to the local newsagent and bought four chocolate bars and a bag of crisps. I ate them all in a matter of minutes because I had just been so incredibly hungry and it had been awful. When I arrived back home I suddenly felt guilty and also greedy for stuffing my face in secret which was exactly what I had done. I felt I had been forced into that situation because my parents were trying to label me with an eating disorder. The doctor was still at the house so I crept up to my bedroom.

It was while I was lying on my bed reading that I suddenly panicked. My parents were sitting in the room below me discussing with a doctor the fact that I was not eating, and here I was having just consumed loads of calories. I just did not know what to do. I didn't want to be ill but I suddenly wondered if I had to be because they thought I was. That night I cried myself to sleep knowing that I would either have to starve or eat in secret. I just could not face the thought of my parents seeing me eat. I would have felt too guilty. After all, they thought I was anorexic.

It was over the next month that I became more conscious of my weight and my appearance. I was embarrassed for anyone to see my figure and so I went out and bought some baggy clothes. I did not want anyone to see my body because I looked normal and they would have expected me to be thin. I had heard my mother on the phone telling friends that she was worried about me because I was not eating and that they had sought medical advice on the problem.

My mother wanted me to go to my own GP but I flatly refused because I knew he would weigh me and say that I was not anorexic. Then I would be embarrassed and I knew I would feel stupid. My Mum assumed that because I did not want to go I obviously did not want to be officially diagnosed as anorexic. It was the total opposite. In the end I was just too fed up of arguing and agreed to go. The worst case scenario happened. The doctor weighed me and I was eight stone. At a height of five foot five inches that is fine. I confirmed that I was having regular periods and he told my mother that there was nothing to worry about. I felt an absolute fool. For the first time I wished he had said I *was* anorexic. Suddenly I could not bear the shame of not being so. My family thought I was anorexic, so did our family friends, and now my close friends from school did too because word had passed round quickly. The grapevine in our town was very strong indeed!

Anger consumed me when I got home and it was not long before I had stormed out of the house. I was angry at everyone and everything but more than anything I felt angry that I was as heavy as eight stone. Suddenly I wanted to be anorexic. I did not want to be that weight anymore, and I also felt a con, a fake, not a real anorexic when everyone, except my GP, thought I was.

The rest of my day was spent in the local library. I found a book on Anorexia Nervosa and read it from cover to cover. I was there for four hours and by the time I left I knew exactly what I needed to do to become anorexic. Basically I had to starve so that my weight dropped so much I lost my periods. Then I would get the official diagnosis.

I refused dinner when I got home. My mother had made me some, thinking that I was no longer anorexic and that therefore everything was back to normal, but it wasn't. I was mad with her, and basically so angry that I couldn't even face food. This starving business was easier than I thought, until about nine o'clock when I was really hungry. I battled with the urge to eat but it just became too overwhelming. In the end I just had to eat. I cycled to the shop once again and this time bought four chocolate bars, a piece of cake and two bags of crisps. I ate them all. When I got home I was suddenly overwhelmed with exhaustion and so I fell straight to sleep.

The next day when I woke up I felt sick and my stomach was bloated. I could not bear it; it felt horrible. I got out my calorie book and calculated that the previous evening I had consumed well over 1500 calories in one go. I felt ashamed. Everyone thought I was anorexic and here I was eating more than ever before. The shame was awful; I couldn't stand it. From then on I developed what I now know to be Bulimia. I was desperate to be anorexic but I just couldn't do it. I just could not starve myself to that extent. I always got too hungry and gave in. I got into a cycle of starving and bingeing which eventually resulted in making myself sick after the binge. The binges got bigger and bigger until they were happening every couple of hours and I was having to steal from shops. I was also eating most of the food in the house. My parents knew nothing about it; they were completely unaware of what was going on. I had three brothers and it was assumed that they were doing all the eating.

I hated it. I felt such a failure because basically I was a failed anorexic. I had also started weighing myself. We had an old pair of scales and on them I was seven and a half stone. I was pleased because I had obviously lost weight. But two weeks later that illusion was ruined. My father threw the scales away and bought a new pair. On them I was eight stone exactly. I was distraught.

I think buying those scales was the worst thing that anyone could have done to increase the problems I was having. Not only did the knowledge of what I really weighed nearly destroy me but those scales were so accurate that I could weigh myself every day and notice if there was even a half pound difference. That resulted in me becoming highly obsessed with my weight and with that came extreme depression.

The depression was obvious to everyone including my doctor. He arranged for me to see a psychologist. My mother told him that I was not eating regularly and that was taken a little more seriously this time so I was referred to a Child and Family Clinic in the area. I was not too bothered about going until four days before and then I began to panic. I was worried sick that these people expected me to be thin when I wasn't so I stopped eating. When the appointment eventually arrived I had not eaten anything for three whole days and my mother told this to the psychiatrist and psychologist that were carrying out the initial assessment.

It was quite an achievement for me to have lasted three days without food, but that time I had been more determined than ever before to do it. I did not want to endure once more the embarrassment I had first undergone with my GP; I was determined to go to the appointment looking ill, and I did. However my plan backfired because they said that I was on the verge of Anorexia. They gave me a diet plan to follow and I realised that all my starving had done was to put me in the same situation I had been in previously – being diagnosed as anorexic when I wasn't.

From then on I ate 700 calories a day but after a while that seemed too much and so I reduced it to 300. It was around that time that my sessions with the psychologist started. I said very little in the first few sessions. Then I started bingeing again. I just found it so hard to stick to a 300-calorie-a-day diet. When the psychologist, Gemma, did ask me about my eating I was too embarrassed to say that I was bingeing. I did not want to tell her that I had been trying so hard to be anorexic and to live up to the label that had been placed on me. So I lied and told her that I was eating 300 calories a day. Gemma then said that I must have been losing weight fast on that. It is that one statement that has always stuck in my head, even now, eight years on. It was after she said that that I suddenly realised that if I really ate 300 calories I would lose lots of weight in a very short space of time. It's quite obvious really but at the time I was so wrapped up in my starving and bingeing cycle that I just didn't think.

Things went gradually downhill after that as I stuck to 300 calories a day. It wasn't as bad as I had expected. After a while I lost the hunger and just felt permanently sick and very weak. I kept having dizzy spells and losing my balance. As for my weight, that just fell off me and I dropped to six and a half stone.

By that point people were starting to get concerned, including my parents. I had managed to hide the weight loss to begin with under baggy clothes but after a while, even under these my weight loss became obvious. It was impossible to hide my face and its protruding cheek bones. Even my hands looked thin and bony, and through my trousers thin bone could be seen when I walked.

My parents contacted the psychiatrist again and said that they needed to see him urgently. We were going on holiday to Spain and they were very concerned about me travelling. They did not want me to lose more weight while I was there and needed to know what to do to prevent this happening. I remember being a little frightened myself about the prospect of the holiday and the effect it would have on my health. I was a little concerned about my weight loss. I was seeing bones that I had never known existed and it was very worrying. For the first time I became frightened of dying. I didn't want to die. I was confused as to what was happening to me and why. So when we went to see the psychiatrist I think I was as relieved as my parents to have the appointment. However the psychiatrist was late and so we did not get an appointment in the end. By the time he arrived he was due to see the next patient and so we did not get to see him.

Looking back now that is the worst possible thing that could have happened. I lost half a stone over the next two weeks and by the time we returned home I was too deep into the Anorexia to want to be helped any longer. The illness had completely consumed me. I was no longer prepared to co-operate with anyone. I no longer wanted help. I just wanted to lose more and more weight. There was no real reason why I wanted to lose weight. I think now I had become addicted to it. Addicted to the high I got from not eating and from seeing the scales go down and down. My health did concern me, it was obvious to me that it was failing fast, but that was not enough to stop me from starving myself. I felt as if I was 'on a roll' and saw no point in ruining it.

More pressure was put on me to eat but I just wouldn't. I was comfortable on 300 calories and I was not prepared to change my routine for anyone. By September I was too ill to start my 'A' level courses and so had to take a year out instead. That was disastrous really. I think if I had gone into the sixth form my studies would have taken my mind off things and might even have given me the motivation I needed to get better. In order to work hard and successfully I knew I needed to eat more. I loved studying and looking back I think there is a strong chance that I would have eaten. As it was I was just given another year to be anorexic.

That year was the bleakest year of my whole life. It was as if it was winter every day. Not only was I permanently cold but the world looked cold and unfriendly. Every day dragged and the fact that I could not sleep made matters worse. I was a mess, a wreck. All of this was because I had been labelled anorexic when I wasn't. It was a self-fulfilling prophecy. I had been treated as an anorexic and so I had become one.

I decided that death was the only way out. I then heard that a girl living in a nearby town had just died of Anorexia. I suddenly felt guilty for being alive and decided if she had died then I had to die. I also decided that if she could do it so could I and set about starving myself to death.

It did not go as planned. When I reached five and a half stone people started getting very concerned indeed. I think they thought I was going to die. I felt absolutely dreadful but thought I would need to be about four stone before I died. I could not understand what all the fuss was about. Then one day my sight started to fail and I was scared stiff. Never before in my life have I ever been that panicked. At the time it was the only thing that could possibly have made me eat more. I ate an extra 100 calories a day from that day onwards. I thought it was a lot and that I would be fine on that but of course I wasn't. My weight continued to drop slowly despite the fact that I was eating so little. My metabolism had obviously slowed down considerably.

The psychiatrist phoned my home every day to see how I was doing. My parents had to weigh me every day and tell him the results. As things were not improving I was told that I would be sectioned in two weeks time if things continued as they were. With that threat hanging over my head I began to think a little more logically. I knew that if I was sectioned I could be given various forms of treatment even without my consent which meant being force-fed even if it was through a naso-gastric tube. Being sectioned would mean that I lost all my rights as a human being. I did not want that so instead I agreed to be admitted.

The hospital I went to had its own adolescent unit so in many ways it was quite pleasant. However I didn't really want to get better. I believe now that sufferers need to live out their Anorexia until they reach the point where they no longer want to have it. For some people that will be as short as a few months, for others years, and for the unfortunate ones decades. Being in hospital definitely saved my life. I developed a serious chest infection. Had I not been in a safe, warm environment I would most certainly have died. I was in hospital for nearly a year. I didn't gain much weight because I was not ready to get better; I just learnt how to be a better anorexic. I learnt tricks of hiding food, burning off calories and making your weight artificially higher on weigh-ins. I learnt all that from the other anorexics that were there. I guess I taught the newer ones when they came in.

Since then I have had five other admissions for Anorexia – it became my life. I have been termed a professional anorexic; what that really implies I don't know, but I guess it isn't something to be particularly proud of. During that time I have seen so many young impressionable anorexics, who are very naive about their illness, join hospital wards. By the time they leave they are experts. There needs to far more control over this as youngsters are becoming damaged for the rest of their lives as a result of this. Hospitalisation can be more damaging than helpful in the long term.

So where am I now? Eight years on I'm still suffering but much of the agony is mental rather than physical. I'm eight stone, the weight I was when I fell ill; at 23 it's a little below normal though not seriously so. I battle with food every day and it still makes my life hell, but I have achieved so much over the last few years. I achieved grade As at 'A' level despite being very underweight. I have just graduated from university. Surviving the three years I spent there is a marvellous achievement, that I graduated is quite out of this world. So I have achieved a lot. I just haven't succeeded in losing my eating disorder, yet.

CHAPTER 17

Anorexia, My Only Friend

'I wanted to get back to normal but I felt I was on a roller-coaster, things had gone out of my control too fast, and I couldn't get off.'

Kirsty speaks of Anorexia as being her best friend. In many ways Anorexia can be viewed in this way. The sufferer feels that they cannot rely on other people and that they are often let down. Anorexia is different, it is with you constantly and you can rely on it being there. When things are bad you can sink into the routine of your Anorexia and you immediately feel better. As a result of this, when people are in recovery, they often miss the companionship Anorexia gave them. They can even go through a long grieving process. But in reality Anorexia isn't really a friend; when you no longer want it there it doesn't always go away, and to finally get rid of it is a long and hard battle, as Kirsty explains.

Even though I like to think of myself as cured from Anorexia now, I still miss it sometimes – I would compare putting Anorexia behind me to losing my best friend. It numbed all my feelings and emotions when I couldn't deal with problems or situations, it was with me 24 hours a day, and it gave me some purpose – something to focus on. I know to 'normal' people that must be a totally insane description of the illness, but maybe I can try to explain what I mean.

I would have described myself as an average 16 year old. I lived at home with my parents and older sister, I did OK at school, I had a few close friends and I'd had a few casual boyfriends. I suppose I appeared a normal, healthy teenager, and all in all I should have been happy and excited about what life held in store for me. I can see that now, but unfortunately at the time I just couldn't cope – all I felt was panic: about my exams; about leaving the security of school life and having to go into the 'real world'; at the thought of having to meet all the new people I would be coming into contact with and about finding a job. Basically I couldn't cope with all the changes that would be happening to me; I just wanted to go to sleep for a while and wake up when all these changes had taken place and I was settled into the routine of my new life.

I can remember lying worrying about this one night and then I thought the answer had suddenly hit me. It was easy – all I had to do was stop eating. That way I could take time out from life for a while and when I had to get back into the swing of things I would be ready for it and be more confident having lost a bit of weight and become more attractive.

It's hard to believe I was so naive but I genuinely believed it to be so simple and straightforward. Overnight I stopped eating. It was amazing – why hadn't I done this before? The weight fell off me and everything else faded into the background. Naturally, my family were very worried and I was dragged along to the doctor. I was taken into hospital for tests to see if there was anything medically wrong with me; obviously there wasn't so I was discharged within a couple of days. I am five foot two inches tall, was eight and a half stone to begin with and was still about seven stone by then, so things weren't at danger level physically.

I had sat my exams by then and was terrified at the thought of having to find a job so it suited me to hide behind the excuse of not being physically strong enough and to have life revolve round psychiatrists and therapists for a while. It wasn't long before I was taken into the young person's section of a psychiatric hospital and I think that's when the fun ended. I wanted to get back to normal but I felt I was on a roller-coaster, things had gone out of my control too fast, and I couldn't get off.

My family were very supportive and when I begged them to take me home and promised to start eating they eventually agreed. Until then I had always been someone who, if I said I would do something, would pull out all the stops to do it, whatever that involved. They were still as naive about the illness as me and wanted to believe that I could cope, with their help, and that now I had promised to get better, I would!

On the outside, for a while, things were normal. I got myself a decent job, I was back at home, went out with old friends, had made new friends at work – basically I appeared to be a happy 17 year old. The reality was the total opposite. All I wanted to do was block out all these new pressures, not have to make any decisions and be able to concentrate on food, calories and exercising 100 per cent of the time. I was steadily losing weight and sinking into deeper and deeper depression. Eventually I cut myself off from everyone; the only friend I had was Anorexia.

It wasn't long before I hit rock bottom and wanted to die, not just escape for a while. By then things were bad. The atmosphere at home was unbearable – I totally ignored my family and locked myself in my room all night. I cut myself off from my friends and physically I was a wreck. The day I was re-admitted to hospital must be one of the worst days of my life. I was rushed into the Accident and Emergency Department at a weight of four stone. I was suffering from hypothermia, my ankles were badly swollen, my veins had collapsed and my blood pressure was so low the doctors couldn't find it; my body had completely closed down. Later I was told that if I hadn't been taken into hospital then I would have been dead within a week.

One thing that still makes me furious is when people ask how my family could have let me get into that state – they have no idea what an anorexic will do, say or promise to get people 'off their back' or what they can hide from people and do to deceive even closest family and friends. If an anorexic does not want help, it is impossible to force it on them. It isn't until an anorexic wants to get better that anyone can do anything.

Like I said, going into hospital that day was one of the worst days of my life, but it was also a turning point. I have always been very stubborn, someone who gives 110 per cent to whatever I am doing, no matter whether trivial or serious. I think being told how ill I was made me realise then that I had given Anorexia 110 per cent of myself. I couldn't have gone any lower without dying. I had said to people 'I've proved you wrong', I could stop eating, could keep losing weight – I'd taken Anorexia to the extreme and I was now ready to give it up.

Fortunately, I didn't realise just how hard the fight ahead of me was going to be. People ask me how I had the will-power to stop eating but that was the easy part compared to the will-power needed to get better. Like I said, the shock of being told how ill I was kicked me into wanting to get better, and for a while that worked but I soon slipped back. I was moved into a psychiatric hospital and had a nurse with me 24 hours a day to make sure I was eating all my meals, wasn't making myself sick and wasn't exercising.

Even now, I can't believe 'experts' thought that this was the answer to my illness. If anything, the six months in this hospital messed me up even more. I was a frightened, scared 17 year old and some of the things I saw and heard I still can't dwell on and don't want to remember. I would agree that I desperately needed professional help, but not to be locked up in a psychiatric ward. I seemed to spend the entire six months feeling scared, crying and begging my parents to take me home. By this time they knew a bit more about the illness and how an anorexic will promise anything to avoid putting on weight and so, after taking advice from the experts, they refused to let me come out.

Even now I can't bear to describe the desperation I felt at being in there – if I hadn't had a nurse with me 24 hours a day I would have tried to kill myself. I also felt totally betrayed – if my parents loved me why couldn't they see the hell I was going through, how could they go back to their comfortable safe home and leave me in there every night?

This created another problem – my fight was no longer just with Anorexia, it was with my parents too. I reckoned Anorexia was still with me, but my parents had deserted me and let me down when I needed them most, so I decided on a new course of action. I would go through the motions of getting better to get out of hospital as quickly as possible, so that I could go home and stop eating again. In my mind this was the best way of hurting my parents and getting back at them for betraying me.

When I was discharged I was just under seven stone and physically 100 per cent recovered but mentally I was at an all-time low. I hated myself, my family and the hospital and had cut all contact with my friends and work colleagues. The only friend I had was Anorexia. It had been the only living thing that had stayed with me and hadn't deserted me when I felt everyone else had!

My aim now was in proving the experts wrong with their view that all I had to do was get up to seven stone to be cured and proving my parents wrong for making me stay in hospital. The only way I knew to do this was to express myself through food, only this time I wasn't the naive 16 year old I had been at the beginning; I was a depressed, scared, deceitful 20 year old whose head was totally messed up. Not only did I cut out food this time but I started taking laxatives as well. Again I was naive enough to believe that they would just help me lose weight faster; I didn't know the whole new set of problems I was letting myself in for.

Gradually I was having to take more and more laxatives, and by the time I was 22 I think I was at my lowest ever, both physically and mentally. I was down to under four stone, I was constantly cold, had headaches and ached all over. I couldn't concentrate on anything and my ankles were swollen again. I couldn't sleep and I was taking over 100 laxatives a day. Obviously it was getting harder and harder to get the amount of tablets I needed but I would still do anything to get them. I even started taking time off my work so I could drive miles to another town to buy them because all my local chemists knew me and refused to sell them to me.

Reading this over, I can't believe I'm describing myself like this, but at the time it seemed perfectly normal behaviour to me. I needed laxatives. I would do anything to get them. I don't know how long things would have gone on like that but they came to a head one day when I ran out and couldn't buy any anywhere. Like I say, I would have done anything to get them and the turning point came when I went into a shop and stole them. I had been brought up in a very religious household and until then had never stolen anything in my life and I think that that was what kicked me into admitting I had to get help. I realised that I was totally out of control.

By this time I had taken to locking myself in my room again as soon as I got home from work, usually for most of the weekend. The only person I could still talk to was my sister who was now married and living away from home. I visited her twice a week and she was the only person I could turn to for help. I think I was more prepared this time for the fight ahead; I knew I couldn't live like this. I had wasted the past six years of my life and now I wanted to beat Anorexia. I also knew that this was it – if I was going to get better I had to commit myself 100 per cent. I wasn't playing games anymore or trying to fool anyone, it was all or nothing.

With my sister's encouragement I got in touch with a friend of the family whose daughter had been anorexic and who I knew was more than willing to offer any help she could. The main thing this time was that I wanted to get better for me, not to get out of hospital or to prove a point, but so I could start living again. By now my parents just didn't know how to deal with me and I think the only way they could keep their sanity, and have some sort of normality in their lives, was to cut themselves off from me, so with just my friend and sister's support and help I gradually came off the laxatives and started trying to build a normal life.

The fight to get better sometimes seemed too much; lots of times I just wanted to give up and I would have if it had not been for the help I got. More than once my sister and her husband had to cancel arrangements at the last minute because I was on a 'downer', and often they had to put up with all my mood swings and shouting, but they were always there, and gradually things started to change for the better. It was a long, hard uphill struggle and I don't know how my sister and her husband and my other friend put up with it. They were on call 24 hours a day. I still cringe when I think of how I was behaving most of the time towards them.

I don't think there was a specific point when I felt I could say 'that's it – I'm cured'; it was very, very gradual. I would have good times when I felt I was getting better and making progress, but then I would have bad days and feel that I had gone right back to square one. Slowly the good days outnumbered the bad, but even now I still have rough days, I suppose all 'normal' people do. The difference now is that I can turn to my family and friends for help through those times.

For the first time in years I would say that on the whole I am happy with my life – I know that if I start to slip back again I will be throwing my life away and I don't think I could ever go through the fight to get better again. That's a frightening thought but I think it's good in a way because it keeps me thinking that I don't want to die. I've got too much to live for now.

CHAPTER 18

The Day Tomorrow Came

'Control that is so controlled it is out of control.'

Many readers will be able to relate to statements such as 'I'll start my diet tomorrow' and 'I'll cut back on my food tomorrow'. It is a sad fact that today's society still places value on thinness. The pressure on both males and females to lose weight is overwhelming. This has resulted in starving being perceived as 'good' and eating 'bad.' More and more children, some as young as eight, are developing this dangerous perception. For Lisa 'tomorrow' did come and with it a desire to lose weight so strong that it became an obsession which completely took over her life.

When I was 24 years old, Anorexia crept into my life – crept in and took it over. I say 'crept', as it came so quietly and stealthily neither myself or anyone else noticed.

I'd always been overweight. As a child, as a teenager, and as a wife and mother. At school I'd sometimes dreamt of what it would be like to be slim like my friends, but not for long. Life was too good. I had plenty of friends and boyfriends, and I did well at school. Everyone told me how nice I was: what a good listener, what good fun, always so confident and organised. I dealt out advice and sympathy by the bucketful. There was no time to diet.

The weight really piled on during my marriage. I was always going to start a diet 'tomorrow.' Tomorrow never came. There were too many other things to think about. I had a young child and a new job, and I had a home to run. However, in April 1989 'tomorrow' did come. Suddenly the time was right. I had to diet, and I knew I would. It was just the next stage of my life. The first couple of weeks were hard – they always are – but this time I knew the self-control would be worth it. Thinking back, that was probably my first, tentative experience of control. Control that is so controlled it is out of control.

Because I had so much weight to lose, I didn't really notice anything for about three months. The scales told me I'd lost weight, but I didn't think I looked any different. I don't think anyone else did either. I tried not to let many people know. I was convinced that they'd only assume that I'd fail again. I just carried on slogging away, just enjoying seeing the needle on the scales going down every week.

By the end of the summer people were beginning to notice, especially friends we hadn't seen for some time. I loved going out wearing new clothes. I loved the compliments. I loved people asking how I did it, then saying they wished they could do it too. In fact I loved it all. At this point I was losing about a stone a month. At this point I also began losing my hair. The first of many trips to the doctor was because of my hair. This was followed by the first of many trips to the hospital. They kept asking me if I was putting on weight. I'd just smile and say 'No!'. When I started to grow hair on my face and shoulders, they suspected Cushings Syndrome. I began a long series of tests, some as an inpatient in hospital. It was easier when people thought I had a physical problem. I kept on losing weight, and losing my hair, but I was happy. This time I had finally got it right. Little did I know how wrong I was.

By Christmas 1989 I looked great. Everyone told me I did, and looking back at the pictures now, I know I did. Looking at the pictures then, I knew that just another few pounds would do it. My Christmas present to myself that year was not to give in to temptation once. I felt so smug and superior when I heard other people moaning about how much weight they had put on over Christmas. I bought new clothes, had my hair cut short, and got myself some new scales.

In the New Year I remember my mum telling me how well I had done, how wonderful I looked, and that now I'd be able to relax my diet. I can remember thinking 'Just one more week'. I remember that so well. I ought to, as I said the same thing *every* week.

At this time I was still going to hospital, as no one could tell me why I was having so many problems with my hair. It never occurred to me to mention my fabulous diet. They might think that had something to do with it. It was at that time that things started to go wrong at home.

My husband had always been a small man, and now he was having trouble eating. Mealtimes became a battleground. I still loved to cook for him and when he didn't finish a meal I'd go berserk. The worst thing was the jealousy. He, who could afford to eat anything he liked, was leaving food, while I craved it so badly but knew I could not have it. I hated him so much for making me feel that way.

It was in the summer of 1990 that he first noticed something was wrong. We had been swimming, and afterwards he told me that I looked thin. The thrill I felt when he said that was overwhelming, but I somehow thought he did not want to hear that and instead I found myself being told I had to see the doctor. I had thought he'd be proud.

Suddenly for the first time I felt fear. It was not a fear of what I was doing but a fear that someone might stop me. The rows over meals had been getting worse. Now they became a nightmare. It was so awful, in particular, for my son. He was only five years old, and didn't understand. All he knew was that Mummy and Daddy were screaming and shouting day in, day out. Even now, at nearly 12, he hates it when we argue. It breaks my heart when I think of what he went through. I was not a mum to him for those couple of years – the only things I shared with him were anger and pain.

The summer was dreadful. My relationship with the rest of the family ceased to exist and my husband got me to see our GP – I hated him and I hated her. I had to go and see her every week to be weighed. I loved that bit. I loved those big, accurate medical scales that went lower every week. I was so happy that I tried to act sorry just for everyone else's sake.

My husband was now frantic. He went to see the doctor on his own, and arranged for me to be referred to a specialist in a couple of months time. For the first time, the word Anorexia was mentioned. I did not believe them. All I knew was that I'd made this brilliant achievement and they wanted to take it away from me. It was around this time that the hospital consultant first questioned my weight loss. While I sat in his office he phoned my GP and told her that I could not wait two months to see a specialist. He then rang the psychiatric department of the hospital and arranged an appointment for the following week. The nightmare was just beginning.

From there began my descent into what I can only describe as hell. Everything was suddenly taken out of my control, so I pushed myself deeper into Anorexia. It was all that was left that was mine. I didn't want them to take it. I didn't have anything else – by then I didn't know anything else. My whole existence revolved around food, and resisting it. Even in my single-mindedness I could see what I had done to my family and I had lost them as well.

I started my sessions with my psychiatrist. It was so upsetting. He wanted to know about my life, my family, everything. I tried to tell him that everything was fine, but it hurt so much. I felt so confused. I didn't know what he wanted me to say. He asked me why I kept losing weight. I told him I had to. He asked me why I felt I had to. I told him I needed the control, that it was all I had. He said that if I didn't stop I was going to die. I told him I was not afraid. I just accepted that it was something that had to happen. It would be a final statement, a testament to my dedication and control, and, at long last, proof that I could really achieve something. By dying, no one would ever be able to take that achievement from me.

I didn't think things could get any worse, but they did. Every time I saw him, he would give me an amount of calories for me to aim to eat every day. I had to keep a diary of what I'd eaten. Every time I lied. Every time I went to my GP to be weighed, I knew that I'd hurt so many people if I had not gained weight. Every time I went I prayed that I'd lost some more. With every thrill I still got from losing another pound, I hurt people I loved so much and I died a little bit more inside.

As Christmas 1990 approached, I thought I was getting near the end. The slightest knock to my legs would make them bleed as my skin was so thin. It was uncomfortable to sit or lie down. I hardly ever slept. I no longer worked as it was an effort to walk. I can remember going to the shops and falling in the road as I could not lift my feet high enough over the kerb. I had to get up stairs on my hands and knees. And the cold – oh, I was so cold. I really thought I would die from the cold.

My whole body hurt, and I was so tired. I just wanted to end it. I think I actually died inside. Seeing my family that Christmas, seeing their pain, broke what little heart I had left. How could I have done this to them? My husband told me later that every time we went to bed, he thought it would be the last time he ever saw me alive.

In January 1991, after much resistance, I finally agreed to go into hospital. At five foot eight inches, and under six stone, the time had come. It's hard to remember much about it except that I felt safe and felt a certain relief. Control over my life had suddenly been taken away from me and I think I was glad. I was just so tired. My body ached and my heart ached, and I knew I couldn't carry on. I guess it is like being in an awful fight with someone, and being beaten senseless. In the end you're glad to be knocked down as at least then its over and someone can come along and start picking up the pieces. It was hard at first, as there is temptation to fight against it, but I gave in. I just couldn't fight anymore. I was initially due to stay a month, but after two and a half weeks I went home. I just wanted to be with my husband and my little boy. I loved them and I needed them. I wanted to start making it right.

CHAPTER 19

My Life in a Chapter

'Your mind has complete control over your whole body; your powers of reasoning are gone; logic and common sense are non-existent.'

Callum's chapter gives out a clear message to magazine editors of the responsibility they have towards the content of their magazines, and the importance of analysing this content in terms of the damage it can have to anorexic and potentially anorexic individuals. These people are not just teenagers and not just females but older people and males also. He considers that these latter categories are overlooked by the media. Editors have the power to make changes. Perhaps Callum's story and the stories of other sufferers will highlight the reasons why they should.

Anorexia for me was like being trapped in a prison where the prisoner is incarcerated in a deep pit and can see daylight above but has no way of reaching it. I was in a tunnel with no light at the end and a train travelling towards me. I would now consider myself recovered but I still live with Anorexia to an extent. I don't think it ever goes away; it is just a case of learning to cope with it. I first became anorexic around the time of my twenty-first birthday. I am now 37 years old.

I have been asked this question so many times by so many different psychiatrists, psychologists and counsellors: 'What do you think caused your illness – what was the trigger?' My answer was, 'I wish I knew'. Was it the fear of growing older and having to leave the easygoing, carefree, happy years of youth and face up to the responsibilities of being a mature male adult? Perhaps I was rebelling against something although I do not see how starving myself would save the whales or bring self-rule to Scotland. Had I done something bad for which God was punishing me? I don't know – I can think of no sane or reasonable explanation as to why I would want to torture my mind and body for so many years and to such an extent that death would have been a welcome relief.

Suffering from Anorexia made me a very selfish, thoughtless and insular person. Everything was about 'me, me, me'. I developed a real chip on my shoulder and never thought twice about the hurt, pain and anguish I was causing to the people around me, particularly those closest to me, which in my case was my family. How my mother and father must have felt to see their son looking this way – what mental anguish and embarrassment must I have caused them? It was not only myself who was suffering from my illness.

My friends made the initial, obligatory noises about how I was not looking well when I first became ill but very soon they became otherwise occupied. With hindsight, however, I can't blame them because no one would really want to have an introverted, bad-tempered and unfriendly individual such as me as a friend. I had undergone a real Jekyll and Hyde transformation. I was convinced I did not need them anyway, and never had. I could cope quite nicely on my own, no problem.

For me one of the worst aspects about my Anorexia, which even now still causes me grief, is the way I treated my family, the lies I told to avoid eating food and the deceitful and hurtful things I did in my single-minded pursuit of losing weight – the birds in our garden were the best-fed in Edinburgh, as were the mice in my wardrobe. All my energies were channelled into that one goal of losing weight – in that pursuit I was tireless. I was never off the bathroom scales and any increase in weight, by the merest fraction of an ounce, was a major disaster and the signal for a renewed bout of dieting and exercising.

I don't think that I will ever be fully able to forgive myself for the way I acted; even now I still get angry with myself for allowing Anorexia to take over and ruin my life. I get the feeling that my brother and sister have never really forgiven me for forcing them to eat when they didn't want to – I always prepared huge meals for them and would sit and watch them eating, getting some sort of perverse pleasure from doing so, from watching their 'suffering', their lack of will-power. I don't blame them at all even now for bearing some deep grudge against me – if either of you should ever read this, I hope you will forgive me.

Anorexia is a difficult condition for non-sufferers to understand and to accept, particularly in a man. But I think the biggest apology must be reserved for my parents, especially for my mum who stuck with me through thick and thin, quite literally. I think she was the only one who had any real idea, however small, of what hell I was going through. More than any other person she helped me to overcome the Anorexia – more so than any of the professionals I saw.

I went to see many 'specialists' during my years of illness but I can't say that any of them really helped me. It was all textbook psychiatry; you were asked the standard questions to which you made the required responses – all a bit of a waste of time really, because I knew full well that I was just saying what they wanted to hear in order for me to get them off my back. A small point that I still remember from my sessions is how each one only lasted the standard hour; sessions would never overrun and anything I had to say after my hour was up would have to wait until the next time.

Anorexia is such an individual and unique illness and can only really be cured from within yourself. I suppose you could say that all sufferers have the cure in their own hands. All right, they (when I say 'they' I am referring to the specialists and it just goes to emphasise the 'me versus the world' kind of attitude I had at the time) can put you on a crash weight-gaining diet and threaten you with hospitalisation and drugs and try to analyse you and find the root of the problem. I do not want to denigrate the skills and experience of these people, but all they really did for me was to provide a friendly and sympathetic ear. Although this certainly helped, with my warped sense of thinking I started asking the question 'what right have they to tell me to put weight on or else?' I became angry with them. It was never me to blame; nothing was ever my fault.

I also became dishonest and deceitful in order to get around their little games. I would strap on ankle weights when it came to weighing times or wear extra clothes in order to reach my 'target' weight for the week. And the lies they forced me to tell – anorexics certainly don't lack imagination!

I would go along to my sessions knowing that we would be covering the same old ground as at my last session. It was like some big game of chess – move and countermove, but it always ended in stalemate because that was the way I wanted it. I did not want to change; I was quite happy with the way things were; there was nothing wrong with me apart from, I believed, being a fat, overweight slob. But if I kept losing weight then everything would sort itself out in the long run – that was what I thought. I somehow argued to myself that by not eating and by losing weight I could avoid facing up to reality and all my problems would just disappear. I was no longer a rationally thinking, or functioning, human being.

It is amazing looking back now at the photographs of myself after I got my weight down from eleven stone to an 'excellent' seven and a half stone, how I could still see myself as fat. It is like looking in one of those funny mirrors at a funfair that totally distorts your reflection. Except with Anorexia you can't just walk away from it. What I saw in the mirror, or thought I saw, was totally different from how I actually looked in reality – I was skin and bones. What is it that can so cloud your vision that you just cannot see what you have done to your body? Your mind has complete control over your whole body; your powers of reasoning are gone; logic and common sense are non-existent.

Many things resulted from my Anorexia – some good (although they were very 'thin' on the ground), most not so good. Anorexia certainly focuses you – you become an achiever, almost to the point of mania. Once you get an idea into your mind you have to achieve that goal – anorexics are very stubborn. I would walk, run, or exercise for hours just to lose those calories and get rid of all the fat, but they never 'dropped off' as they had promised in those magazines' diets. So to get around this problem, I just had to eat even less and exercise even more – although I was physically exhausted, at least I was fit.

The most important thing that came out of my Anorexia, and was probably the turning point for me, was going to university and getting my degree – this was the light at the end of the tunnel which had finally appeared and felt within reach. I was committed to doing well. I refused to fail at anything. Starvation was the punishment for failure. My studies gave me something to channel all my thoughts and energies into. I would quite happily study for hours on end – the perfect student. My degree still gives me great satisfaction because it proves that I am not a totally useless human being – I wish I could prove this to myself more often. I'll just have to do another degree.

Food is no longer the issue it once was although I still have very low self-esteem; the problems that caused my illness are still there. As to whether I am cured, the question is: are recovered anorexics, like reformed alcoholics, ever really cured? For alcoholics, it just takes the one drink to tip the balance. The same applies to us. It just needs one inadvertent statement about you putting on weight or missing the odd meal here and there, and before you know it you are back to square one, and the agony of recovery begins again. Anorexia is always hanging over you. Even today, I admit, I am not totally cured of my Anorexia but I do have it under reasonable control. Food still plays an important part in my life but it does not now totally control or dominate it. I can happily eat chocolate or take milk in my coffee without being overcome with guilt. I no longer have to check the calorie value of everything before I eat it and, thankfully, I don't consume large amounts of laxatives anymore. I have my diet worked out to an acceptable level; I don't have three meals a day but when I do eat I enjoy it. My fitness training programme allows me to feel that I have exercised enough to lose an acceptable number of calories and burned off those extra few pounds that somehow appear on my body overnight, although I mainly exercise now for the enjoyment it gives me.

I am able to admit to myself now that I had, and still have I suppose but to a much lesser extent, an eating disorder. But doesn't everyone have some sort of eating problem? Food is such an influential, integral and controlling factor in our lives – it rules you whether you consciously know it or not. Most people will see their normal day revolve around food to some extent. When you are hungry the pangs override everything else and you can only think straight again once you have satisfied that hunger with food. By ignoring this most basic human need you cannot move on to satisfy your other needs.

Meals are taken at regular times of the day. Magazines tell us, 'Don't eat such and such a food because it's bad for you' or 'Follow this particular diet regime if you want to live longer'. Television adverts are full of beautiful people like whom we can aspire to be if we drink a certain mineral water or use this or that type of shampoo. And, no matter how much you deny it, everyone is influenced to varying degrees by what they read in the media or see on television. How we should lead our lives, how we should think, how we should look – all these factors are increasingly being manipulated for us, supposedly in our own interests. Media hype and pressure must, I feel, be seen as a contributory factor towards Anorexia nowadays.

As far as male Anorexia is concerned it is greatly overlooked by the media, along with older female sufferers too. To me this just seems like another example of the lack of thought put into reporting by the media. They give a completely false impression – that Anorexia is only suffered by teenage females – and they are very wrong. Maybe I am being too cynical but I do feel that I am justified as males do suffer from Anorexia as well; however, because all the books and magazine articles seem to ignore this fact completely males believe that they are all alone in their suffering. We labour under the impression that we are freaks – for your average, red-blooded male admitting to having a 'female only' problem is definitely not macho. So you just have to bottle it up inside and pretend to yourself, and to the rest of the world, that no problem exists.

It can no longer be argued that there are no magazines aimed at the male market because over recent years several have become available, yet those publications rarely touch on the subject of male Anorexia. The models in the adverts or fashion pages, like their female counter-parts, are always slim – we are back to this problematic portrayal of beautiful successful people as also being super-slim and well built. Mr Average or people over 30 need not apply!

Male models always have V-shaped torsos, rippling muscles and are usually unshaven. And, although it is not 'hip' to admit it, we all aspire to look like the models in the clothes adverts or the muscle bound 'hunks' demonstrating how you can have a body like they have by working out in the gym for only 15 minutes a week. So, indirectly, we males are being consciously manipulated into believing that thin is beautiful. As well as the adverts in the actual magazine you just need to glance at the classified adverts section at the back where you find advertisers offering to change or enhance any and every part of your body to make you more beautiful – do people really go in for liposuction? Have we really become that vain and naive?

But we keep coming back to this problem of 'image' – a male cannot easily come out with 'oh, by the way, I'm on a diet' or start drinking diet cokes when he is out with the lads. It just does not work – a prime example of peer pressure in everyday action. A similar corollary is that males don't cry, we leave that up to the female. How totally warped and misguided this belief actually is. If only males could admit to themselves that it is quite acceptable to cry then maybe the species in general would be a lot more relaxed with themselves and how they appear to others.

I feel that given the influence that magazines in particular have over their audience in so many facets of their individual lives it should now become their responsibility to focus on more important issues, such as male Anorexia, rather than churning out the same old mundane features month after month on how to chat up women, or recover from a hangover. Editors have a unique opportunity here to change the entire format of their magazines, and all for the better.

My message to them is to publish articles and features that are contemporary, relevant and worthwhile and will achieve some good, to let their male readership know that Anorexia is not something to be ashamed of, and that there are other sufferers out there. Encourage males to forget the stereotypical image that they are meant to be aspiring to, and to get the notion out of their minds that by failing to comply with these conditions they are not qualifying as 'real' men. It is perfectly acceptable to go out for a coffee and a chat, or to push a trolley round a supermarket. Every social get-together does not have to revolve around how many pints of lager can be consumed. Looking at pictures of models in fine suits and fancy shirts is all very well, but these clothes are always well outside the everyday budgets of the majority of readers. Concentrate instead on the more affordable and everyday items. Bring some realism to the whole subject.

Going back to my own experience of Anorexia, what is the legacy left after my own suffering? Physically, I am still slim and find it difficult to eat a large meal. My appetite has never fully recovered and I don't really experience hunger pangs as such. I am also a 'lonely' eater and dislike eating in public, avoiding it as much as possible.

I still have to be active all the time and walk everywhere, along with my daily sessions at the gym. But an adverse result of my insatiable desire to exercise and in particular to run is that my body is now racked with injuries that steadfastly refuse to clear up. My back, in particular, gives me a great deal of bother and my joints, especially at the hips, knees and ankles, cause me a lot of pain. Even when injured I would carry on training knowing full well that by doing so I was making the injuries much worse. Injuries that would have only been temporary hindrances in a healthy body have now taken full-time residence in my body; even now I have not learned my lesson and I persist in training.

At the end of the day I believe that there are no real differences between the female and male anorexic. I have read countless publications and articles over the years, always referring to Anorexia as a female-only disorder, but in the majority of cases I can completely relate to the sufferer and their description of the illness. I have suffered from the general symptoms described and I can understand all of the more individual symptoms experienced – even when they are expected to be suffered by females only. It does not matter which age, sex or social class you are, eating is a common factor, and potential eating disorders too. The only real difference between the two is the openness, or lack of it in the male case, that the anorexic displays.

I think, for me personally, this lack of openness and fear of becoming an outcast led to my being a 'late' developer of Anorexia; the symptoms could have been there but I just made a good job of hiding them. I suppose also there was the fear of being laughed at and ridiculed because I was seeing a psychiatrist. All mental illnesses carry such a stigma. It is seen as a sign of weakness, of not being in control or able to manage your own life. But how wrong this idea is because no one can display more control over their life, or be so strong-willed and, at the same time, so narrow-minded towards reality, as the anorexic.

Mentally, I still get extremely depressed and have deep feelings of hopelessness and despair and self-loathing; I can also be extremely irritable. It may not sound like it but I am definitely a lot better than I used to be.

There is hope. That is the message I would like to give out to all sufferers and their friends and families. The road to recovery from Anorexia is a very long and difficult one, but it can be made, and when you reach the end you will realise it was well worth the effort. Good luck!

List of Contacts

The Eating Disorder Association
Sackville Place
44 Magdalen Street
Norwich
Norfolk NR3 1JU
Telephone Helpline: 01603 621414
(Monday–Friday, 9 am–6.30 pm)
Youth Helpline: 01603 765050
(Monday–Friday, 4 pm–6 pm)
Fax: 01603 664915

The Eating Disorder Association (EDA) is a national charity offering help, support and information to people whose lives have been affected by eating disorders, in particular, Anorexia and Bulimia Nervosa. It aims to campaign to improve standards of treatment and care and to raise awareness of eating disorders and related issues. The range of services offered by the EDA include: telephone helplines, support through membership of EDA including newsletters and conferences, a network of locally based groups and individual volunteers who offer a 'listening ear' by telephone and letter. They also publish information about eating disorders including the professional journal, *European Eating Disorders Review*, and guidelines on service specifications for the treatment of Anorexia and Bulimia Nervosa.

The Eating Disorder Support Network
Rosemary Shelley
50 South Park Avenue
Mansfield
Nottinghamshire NG18 4PL

The Eating Disorder Support Network (EDSN) is free to join and links sufferers on a national scale. Members receive a database of sufferers to whom they can write for support and advice. A free newsletter, *Network News*, is also produced for members every quarter. EDSN welcomes sufferers with any kind of eating problem, at any stage in the illness and of any age. Contact the above address for further details. No telephone calls please.

Anorexia and Bulimia Care (ABC)
Northern and Administration Office
15 Fernhurst Gate
Aughton
Ormskirk
Lancashire L39 5ED

Anorexia and Bulimia Care (ABC) is a Christian organisation offering help to sufferers of Anorexia, Bulimia and Compulsive Eating and their carers. The organisation was set up out of a desire to combat the negativity which surrounds these diseases and to show that there is an answer – it is possible to live a renewed life, totally free of eating disorders. Please contact ABC at the above address. The organisation does not discriminate if you do not have Christian beliefs.

Centre for Eating Disorders (Scotland)

Mary Hart
3 Sciennes Road
Edinburgh EH9 1LE
Telephone: 0131 668 3051
Fax: 0131 667 9708
e.mail mhart@globalnet.co.uk

The Centre for Eating Disorders (Scotland) has a special interest in starving and bingeing conditions, obesity, those recovering from Anorexia who can maintain a stable weight, and Bulimia Nervosa. They recognise that eating disorders are symptoms of underlying problems which may include: depression and low self-esteem, feelings of loss, loneliness, anxiety and panic attacks, posttraumatic stress and sexual and physical abuse. Their working methods include: individual therapy, couple and marital work, family therapy, stress management and symptom management.

Diet Breakers

Mary Evans Young
Barford St. Michael
Banbury
Oxon. OX15 OUA
Telephone: 01869 337070
Fax: 01869 337177

Diet Breakers unites people of all sizes, backgrounds and professions to challenge and recover from the diet mentality and have a healthier lifestyle.

The organisation is best equipped to work with people to avoid eating disorders, or those in recovery. They run workshops around the country on improving body image and help promote National No Diet day (6th May each year) the object of which is to celebrate individuality, self-acceptance and a healthy lifestyle. Members of Diet Breakers get discounts on many support materials and workshops plus five issues of the organisation's magazine.

National Osteoporosis Society

PO Box 10
Radstock
Bath BA3 3YB
Telephone: 01761 471771
Fax: 01761 471104

The National Osteoporosis Society works exclusively to improve the diagnosis, treatment and prevention of osteoporosis. The society provides advice, information and support throughout the UK. It is an independent and unbiased organisation with its own specialist medical advisers.

Al-Anon Family Groups UK and Eire

61 Great Dover Street
London SE1 4YF
Telephone: 0171 403 0888
(24 hour Helpline service)

Al-Anon offers understanding and support for families and friends of problem drinkers, whether the alcoholic is still drinking or not. Alateen, a part of Al-Anon, is for young people aged 12–20 who have been affected by someone else's drinking, usually that of a parent.

For details of meetings throughout the UK and Eire please contact the above.

Bristol Crisis Service for Women
PO Box 654
Bristol
BS99 1XH
Telephone: 0117 925 1119 Fridays/Saturdays 9 pm–12.30 am

The Bristol Crisis Service for Women aims to offer help and support to females who are victims of sexual abuse, suffer from Anorexia, or harm themselves by cutting.